JANE MAST MOORE

# He Carried Me

PRESS

# Acknowledgments

Special thanks to all who held me up the prayer as I was planning and working on this book. To Chris and Dan Diener , to Chris who is my editor of this book as well as a friend, and Dan has been a very wonderful spiritual advisor as well as friend, without your encouragement it would have been much harder to write the book. Also to Wayne Summers who had the courage to tell me that God had something special for me to do, and the unwavering encouragement that he gave me to stick with it, that it was going to be worth it all, and many will be helped. Also Aunt Betty Kauffman who shared her memories with me.

# DEDICATION

This book is dedicated all secret survivors. Being a secret survivor is very difficult yet with the Lord's help we can make it and we can be healed. Though we may never forget the incident, the pain, the feeling that we are not loved. Yet there is one who will carry us, and love us. The heavenly Father loves us more than any earthly father. Though it may be hard to comprehend this after the abuse that we have suffered, He is a very loving Father we just have to believe. Just remember abuse in any form be it physical, mental, sexual is not right, and God did not put you here to be a punching bag in any way shape or form. The person who is abusing you, or has abused you does not love him/herself

Also this book is also dedicated to the memory of my precious grandmother, THERSA HOS TETLE R, who taught me the love of reading books, writing, and music.

# Preface

$\mathcal{T}$his is a story of my life. It is the story of how it all began. It is the stone tossed into the water, that rippled out for years and years to come. I have written this book in just how it is going to work for good. But He chose me to go through what I have, because He knew I could deal with it. God did not give me the Rumatoid Arthritis, Fibromyalgia, congestive heart failure, the Atrial Fiberlation. He allowed it. The devil gave it to me, he wants to kill and destroy the Father's children.

# Chapter 1

*M*om's mother Bessie decided she could not continue to take care of her five children. So she packed up Ruby, Sarah (Marie), John, Della, and Lester, taking them to the Mennonite Children's Home in West Liberty, Ohio. The children were naturally upset as ever being ripped from their home. They gave her a hard time as to where and why they were going. The only response she gave them was that she could not deal with them anymore. She later told them that their dad was ill and she could not handle them and the other children still at home. The children promptly announced loudly that the man was not their father. That their father was dead. Bessie told them again that she could not take care of all of them, that they would just have to buck up and deal with it.

As they got closer to the Home the children's fear in increased. When the Home came into view they saw a large red brick building, two stories high. There was plenty of grass and trees in the yard and a big sign that said, Mennonite Children's Home, (mom always called it the Sunshine Children's Home). The information I found on it showed this was not ever the name. So I am not sure where that name came from. The children and Bessie walked into the building to the reception hall, they were greeted by the matron of the home. Bessie explained the situation, and also the children could be foster or adoptive children.

The children that were old enough to do chores were given chores to do. Sarah was given dishwashing duties. She hated it, as they always made the dishwater hot. However she would soon got used to it. With so many children in the home there was little bonding with the adults, only the other children. The whole yard was available for playing, and the one tree that gave them the most shade in summer was a favorite place to play. It was on a small hill, and that was the spot where Sarah Marie played nurse. I would find this out when I was in my 40s, that this was why she pushed me into being a nurse. I wanted to be a beautician, and mom later admitted that if she had known how the beautician business would grow she would have let happen that I could have been a beautician instead of a nurse.

Meanwhile in Indiana, and a minister and his wife, Amos and Thersa Hostetler were suffering the loss of the daughter born breech who died at birth. They would lose a total of five children to death. To be with them you would never have a clue of the great loss they had suffered over the years. They knew of the Mennonite Children's Home which was just hours away in Ohio. They begin to think and pray about finding a child that needed a home and the love of parents. They decided to go and see who they felt would be the best fit for their family. The first time they visited the home they met nine-year-old Sarah Marie, and brought her home as a foster child. After Papa's death in 1993 mom found adoption papers, she had not known until then that she was adopted. Sarah Marie was so crushed by the rejection of her birth mother that she never recovered, she would never be able to completely permit someone fully into her heart. It was hard for her all her life, even her own children would not feel the love from her that they needed and wanted. Only in the very latter years of her life would she occasionally say "I love you."

While at the Home she learned how to clean and polish furniture, wash windows, and dishes. Her new mom was surprised how much she had learned. She called her new parents Mama and Papa, also informing them her name was Marie, that she did not like the name of Sarah. A family that lived just 1 mile from her and attended the same church had chosen her sister Ruby. Therefore, they spend a lot of time together. Ruby's foster father was very abusive, so much so that she wanted to run away. It had come to be that all of the children would end up in the same area, and they were able to keep in touch with each other over their entire adult lives.

At one point in time Ruby's abuse was so great that she and Marie planned to run away. Betty, another foster child of Mama and Papa's, knew of the plans and was so upset she told Mama and Papa. She did not want to lose her sister. Papa felt that Fhinis, Ruby's foster father, should know, so Marie, Betty and Mama went along with him to have talk about the problem. To the total shock of the Hostetler family, Fhinis took off his belt and beat Ruby with it a number of times. Betty was beside herself at the occurrence as she had told Papa. But she did not want to lose her sister, whom she loved dearly. Ruby would marry a wonderful man and raise five children. We cousins always enjoyed getting together no matter the time of year, we always enjoyed our time together. For Ruby her scars were with her all her life too.

One day Mama, Betty, and Marie were sitting in the living room when all at once Mama smelled smoke and looking up she saw that the chimney was on fire, it was red-hot. It looked like there was a fire in the upstairs so quickly, she told Marie to run down to the neighbors and call the fire department. She and Betty stayed at the house and begin carrying things out as quickly as they could. Betty told me that every time she took something out she would yell FIRE! Neighbors came from all around to help get things out of the house. The fire department came to the house and the fire was quickly put out. The two men who carried the piano out of the house, were unable to carry it back in. They needed more help. After everything settled down Mama went about cleaning up the mess and Papa repaired the area that was burnt.

Unbeknownst to Mama, Papa had been looking for a piano at the different sales that were going on in the area. One day he went off and didn't tell anyone where he was going. When he returned later that day he was soon followed by a wagon with a large item on the back. He did not say a word as the men pulled up to the house to unload the large item. To the delight of the women of the household it was the much desired piano. As soon as it was in place Mama sent down and started playing. That same piano is still in the family today, and as I look at it I remember Mama playing the midnight fire alarm, although I loved to hear her playing that song it was a fast moving song and at times she would say she couldn't play because the arthritis was hurting too much that day. But my fondest memories of that piano as a child growing up are either listening to Mama play, or all of us joining around the piano and she played while we sang. These are such precious, precious memories which I shall never forget.

# Chapter 2

The girls thrived and grew on the farm. Papa was a minister, schoolteacher, and carpenter, he also farmed. He taught in a one-room school all of his teaching years. I remember how he wanted to teach Mama to drive and he felt that the Pashan schoolyard was the perfect place for her learn. She got behind the wheel, got into gear, and started to go in a circle. She wanted to stop and had forgotten what she had been told as to how to stop, so she kept going in circles yelling for Papa to help. He was yelling that she needed to push on the brake. Somehow the car was stopped, and Mama said she would never drive a car again and she never did.

Mama was a fantastic cook, and baker, and candy maker. One never left the table hungry when she cooked. She could play the piano, compose music and arrange and rearrange music. She instilled the love of music and singing in all of her children. She also loved nature, and had the greenest thumb in the area. She had the most beautiful Iris, and pollinated plants for new colors. She loved lilacs too, there were huge bushes loaded with lots of blossoms every spring. She was a great seamstress, making all of her own clothes. She chose print dresses for casual wear and chose the plain darker colors for Sunday with a cape over the bodice. She wore her Mennonite covering daily as she felt this was what the Scripture called for. She wore her hair combed straight back and bun at the nape of her neck. She loved to read and write about the youth activities of the church, some of her writings are in a collection in the in the Goshen College, Goshen, Indiana historical archives. One thing about both of Papa and Mama they love the Lord unfailingly, they believed the old saying: " a family that prays together stays together." Mama was a great prayer warrior and it showed in her compassion for others. She was also a cancer survivor though it would repeat and take her life at age 68. Papa was an awesome teacher, he never preached he taught. I enjoyed hearing granddaddy, as I called him, preach the Sunday service. He made it so interesting you didn't mind sitting there as a child listening. Granddaddy was not tall man, wore glasses, had piercing blue eyes, if you did something wrong those eyes would nail you in a second, no words were needed to be spoken. The grandchildren loved to come to come granddaddy's house, especially in the summer.

One time Mama heard something messing with her hen with chicks just outside the back door. In a flash she grabbed a broom, flew out the door, and with one good swat hit the culprit in the hind end. As it ambled across the yard she saw that it was a skunk! It just kept going and did not spray her. Sometime later Marie would come in from the woods telling Mama that she had found a kitten she had petted it, and it had a white stripe down its back. She was promptly informed that it was a skunk and what could happen to her if the skunk was annoyed. On a picnic in the woods one day with Mama and the girls saw a skunk. Marie wanted to pet it. And Mama again patiently explained that the kitty was not a kitty it was a skunk, and if it sprayed they would all be very sorry.

When Sarah and Betty came to dating age, which was age 16, Papa had strict instructions for them. They could not go out on a date with any boy who did not come to the door and knock. Also upon returning, they could not sit in the car for any longer than five minutes, any longer would lead to problems for both of them. If it lasted longer than five minutes it was like on happy days, the light flickered off and on. These dating instructions were received like any teenager would receive them. They were not thrilled. But they knew to obey or else they would not be dating. And Papa's blue eyes said it all.

The girls learned with Mama's supervision how to cook, bake, plant a garden, and care for it. They also learned in the fall the art of canning the fruits of their hard summer's labor, even how to sugar cure a ham, and hang it in the cold attic to cure.

# Chapter 3

$\mathcal{A}$ t that time a young man from New York made appearance in the area. His name was John Paul, he was 16 years old. He had been born in Shipshewana, Indiana, then his parents had decided to move back to New York State. He preferred the name Paul instead of John. He had run away from home. His mother Katie had died of complications after gallbladder surgery. Katie's mother and Thersa's father were brother and sister. So Paul felt comfortable coming here. He just could not deal with the way his father treated him. Paul was very close to his mother, he had been unhappy before she died, but when she died he could not take it anymore. He was quickly accepted into the family. He found work at the Rainbow Lake Inn (also known as Shore Lake) as a waiter. One of the employees there was a relative and offered him a place to stay which he quickly accepted. He became friends with Marie and Betty. Paul loved to laugh and play jokes on people. So it was never boring when he was around

Paul and Marie started to date, but she was dating another boy also. His name was Walter. He also went to the Emma Mennonite church with his family. Papa and Mama did not care for him and had warned Marie that if she married Walter she would have a very miserable married life so she stopped dating him and dated Paul exclusively. Mom told me this story of one day. She and Paul were double dating with some friends, they were in the back seat and Paul began to kiss her then stuck his tongue in her mouth. At that precise moment they hit a bump in the road and she bit! He let out a howl, and everyone in the front seat one to know **what** was going on back there. 'She bit me" came the reply. I thought O UCH! I did not know what French kissing was at that time.

The day finally came when Paul asked her to marry him and she said yes. On February 24, 1940, they were united in marriage by Bishop S. C. Yoder, in Goshen, Indiana. It was a small wedding. Marie wore a simple white dress that Mama had made for her. She had a corsage of white roses. Paul wore a white shirt and a dark suit. Only family and friends attended the cozy living room wedding. It was not long after they were married Marie found out that she was expecting. She and Paul were thrilled to tell the family. Paul was working for Honey Crust Bakery, he drove the panel truck and made deliveries. The neat thing about the bread truck coming was the fact they had a freezer on board, and you could buy an ice cream for five cents. When I was a child the truck always had the most wonderful aroma with the baked goods on board.

Paul left the bakery truck route to drive an oil tanker. Driving truck has been a Mast thing to do. Father, and two sons drove truck both long-haul and short distances. I recall stories that Grandpa Mast told about driving in the Philadelphia Hills. I recall once when he had a rider with him, of course he had to show off and scare the poor man into next year. He thought it was so funny. I never did see what was so funny about scaring someone so bad.

Mom got pregnant again and things were progressing nicely, when she got the flu. So she took some medication to help her with the flu. But she had a miscarriage and it seemed that the medication is what did it. Mom and Dad dealt with the situation as they knew how. They pulled themselves up by their bootstraps and worked through the sorrow.

Marie and Paul decided to get a cat it helped fill the void that was left when Paul was working. One day they had company. The cat as cats do came in to see who was there, but then decided to sit down and take a bath washing its tusshie tail. Paul was mortified. How could that cat do that with company visiting! Marie patiently explained the cats didn't do it to shame him, all the while trying not to laugh.

In June, 1941, Marie went to the doctor. She could hardly wait for Paul to come home to tell him the wonderful news. Another baby was on the way! Paul was over the moon with joy! He picked up Marie and spun around in his joy. Paul love to go dancing, there was a dance one night and he decided to go to it. Marie was brought up to believe it was sinful to dance so she never went. Instead, she went into labor and she was rushed to the Sturgis Memorial Hospital. Paul was told it would be hours until the baby would be born. So he felt there would be plenty of time to go to the dance and make it back before the baby was born. But I had other ideas, and at 8:30 I entered the world. The first thing my dear daddy said of me when he saw me was "she's all nose"! Then he laughed and picked me up. Six months later he kissed mom and I goodbye. He still had to deliver a load of oil, it was a Sunday maybe he could get the load delivered maybe he could get back in time for church that evening. It was a day to change all of our lives. He had put an application for work with the as a railroad conductor. They were both anxiously awaiting for the reply. It came one day too late.

As Daddy was driving down the road he decided to pass a slower vehicle, he started to pass then realized there was an oncoming vehicle and he did not have enough time to pass the vehicle he trying to pass. His front axle broke as he was slowing down, and caused the oil tanker to jackknife. It was sitting precariously on this small ditch. Apparently he thought he was okay and could climb down on the cab. As he got out of the cab and stood beside it, it suddenly fell on him

Mom was at home with me thinking all was okay, we were living at the Shipshewana Lake. It would be 7 PM that night when a state trooper arrived to give the news to mother. She called granddaddy and Mama, which is what I called grandma, to come over and stay with her for a while. They knew very well the sorrow of the loss of a loved one, and were a great help to mom. I was only six months old when my daddy died I remember him by a few pictures which I cherish dearly.

Sometime after daddy's death mom decided to go to Buffalo, New York where Uncle Junie, and Aunt Rosetta lived in a small one bedroom apartment. Mom looked for work finally finding it on a large horse farm. She was the house-keeper for the couple, mom said the couple treated me like a grandchild. I really believe that's where I learned my love of horses. Sometime later mom decided to return to Indiana where she began dating Walter again. This was another time that words were spoken previously regarding the subject or someone and words were ignored. I find it interesting how something someone else has done will ripple out to affect you. It's like throwing a pebble in the pond the rings go out and out and out and out till they can't go any further, the same is true with relationships. How often have you heard someone say it will not hurt anyone else? But the opposite is true your deci-sions can and will affect people whether you know it or not. From here on the story starts to change, the ripples hit myself, my sister and my brothers. We are still affected to this day by the ripples when that decision was made.

# Chapter 4

*B*efore mom remarried, Uncle Junie and Aunt Rosetta made an offer to mom. They offered to adopt me rather than have me be a burden to my mother. Back then the woman stayed home, she did not go out into the workplace like we do now. So she had no skills other than housekeeper. But mom refused she said she could not give up her child. Another ripple has come in this ripple that will be devastating.

After a time mom started to date she dated several men, but ended up marrying the one that Granddaddy and Mama had told her not marry. And the prediction that was made before mom married my daddy, came true. They were married in November 1944, to this union a girl, and two boys were born. When she was pregnant with her last child, he took her to the hospital and told the staff he would be back on Sunday. He had too much farm work he had to do, and he turned around and left the hospital, returning as he said Sunday.

I remember my mother was expecting my sister Judy, I was walking around telling everybody that I would have a baby sister born on my birthday. They would pat me on the head and smile and say how precious. But my baby sister was born on my birthday. I think of that so often and I have to laugh at all these people that thought I didn't know what I was talking about. Living with my stepfather was no picnic. I recall I wanted to see some pictures that were housed under the stairs in the living room. I was scared to death to open that door because you could hear the rats gnawing on wood somewhere. But he insisted that I could open that door and go in that dark to get what it was I wanted, the picture album. I grabbed the picture album as quickly as I could and closed the door. I had heard mother getting on him for making me go into that closet. But he could care less. Another time I am not sure how old I was, he sent me back to Lane to bring the cows up from the field. I looked in the field he said they were in but they were not there. I looked in another field and they weren't there either. Finally I decided to return back to the house. He and mom were standing at the gate. It was a big wooden gate that was big enough to have tractors and horses and every-thing else go through. I did not want to climb over the fence because I had a blister on my hand and I knew if I crawled over the I would end up breaking my blister, not my idea of fun. He threatened to beat me with the black snake. That freaked me out even more, the black snake was a long black whip that when cracked or snapped was extremely scary. Mom told him to open the gate but he refused again, so I had to climb over the gate broke my blister and went into the house with mom to put something over the blister. I knew that this man did not love me, but I so wanted a father's love, I was so hungry for a father's love. Another time it was shortly after mother had given birth to my brother. Since he was a newborn, and she could not pick up anything of weight yet, she had noticed that the stove in the bedroom was very hot, I lay very close to the stove, and she wanted him to pick me up and get me out of that bedroom. He refused he said I was fine and he was not going to carry me out, this was in the middle of the night. Mom said she did not when she know when she had prayed so hard for something because she knew if God did not intervene she would lose another child.

I loved living on the farm the cows, horses, the pigs not so much, and the cats. One evening I was helping spray the cattle for flies that had come in to be milked. I was spraying away not paying much attention to the cow next to me I had my back to her when she decided she wanted to move closer to me. The way I was bent over my head was towards the cow that I was spraying, I thought the other cow had moved back until to my great surprise, and indignation, she ever so carefully lifted her tail and made a lovely deposit upon my head. I got out of that barn as fast as I could, I was so embarrassed I could have died 1000 times.. I made my way to an area between the old summer kitchen, and the old smokehouse. Mom was in the garden with the hired girl. I called to her to come to me. She told me to come onto the garden I refused saying that I needed her. She asked what the reason that she had to come was. Then I told her that the cow had pooped on my head! So she came laughing from the garden her and the hired girl both. I had my hair in braids so she got the hose and started to rinse my head off, then she got the shampoo and started to shampoo my head. That was one incident I have never forgotten in all my 72 years. I remember another time when I was younger when grandpa and dad were milking cows, they had a bucket of milk sitting out and then run it through the strainer and into the can. They were talking and I was standing there and for some reason I decided to back up and landed in the pail of milk. As they roared in laughter they told me to go into the house so mom could put something else on me. Moe was just a baby in diapers. So mom decided since I had no panties there I had to wear one of Moe's diapers, I was mortified that there was no way out my dress was and panties were soaked and I needed to have some clothes on to go home, as we lived close to Shipshewana.

Another thing I do know, when we were living in the house over close to Shipshewana, was I wanted to tap the tree for some sap. Also, we would go in to the chicken house to gather eggs. And there he was in all of his glory slowly walking on towards us. In the summer we went barefoot. So our ankles were always exposed to whatever Mr. Rooster wanted to do. He would attack and run, then return for another attack if he could. It was an ongoing battle with that nasty rooster. Also in the summer we had enjoyed picking strawberries, not only to eat out in the garden but also to put in for the winter. One day I walked out into the strawberry patch and was looking for some red ripe strawberries. As I was looking all of a sudden I saw a snake! I let out a war hoop, mom and dad came running to get the snake! But by the time they got there the snake was no longer seen I guess my scream scared it off.

We had wonderful woods on the farm. I still love walking back down to the lane to the woods. One time walking back there I saw mother raccoon and her two babies. All they were so cute I just stopped dead in my tracks I did not want to disturb her so stood very still till mama and the babies ambled away. We also had an area named Crane airport. It was a pond and a part of woods, there were fallen trees and dead trees where the Crane fly in and make their nests in the summer. We always stayed very quiet as we watched. It was so neat to see those cranes flying in to Crane airport with their long legs dangling behind them. The woods was full of flowers and different trees. It is fun to walk through the woods to just be alone with God.

One day a little black and white cocker spaniel wandered into our yard, all of us kids were just nuts about her especially me. I named her Patsy and we had more fun with her. One day she delivered puppies in the barn my stepfather did not like the puppies around so he killed them. Then wanted to show the puppies to us kids, mom had an absolute hissy was not about to let him do it. Patsy blamed the cows in the stanchion for killed her puppies, and she attacked the cow closes toer. The next time she was having puppies she went and hid them under the front porch. He proceeded, tell mom when he found out about the puppies she had to get rid of them that day. She took Patsy and the puppies, and the kids that were in school, and tried to find the Elkhart humane shelter, but could not find, so she dumped Patsy in the puppies off in front of someone's house and left. I was devastated when I heard what had been done to Patsy puppies I used to pray for that dog many many times as a child just hurt so bad that this could happen to very sweet dog.

When I was in the third grade I had Mrs. Bevington for a teacher, she had white hair and a way about her you just knew she came over and they are she was that old. For some reason she just took a dislike to me and of course my mother. She would call me up to the desk just about every day and the moment I got to the desk she didn't care who was around she would tell me I smelled very bad. I knew this wasn't true because mother was a stickler for wearing clean clothes and being clean when you went to school. Every day this would go on I hated. I did not want to be stuck. It was at the end of the third grade. It was in the summer, mom and the three other kids and I were standing in the kitchen. I do not recall the conversation, all I remember is whatever I said made my mother turn white as a sheet. She told me to watch the other three kids, she opened the stairway door turned around and said, " I have to go pray." I had told my mother that I was being molested by my stepfather. When she came downstairs she told me that I was going to live with granddaddy and mama. I did as I was told and went upstairs to pack my things. I was excited I was going to live granddaddy and mama. I remember arriving and granddaddy's mother was sitting in her usual chair kitchen and mom made some remark to her. I don't know what she said. She then told me to go upstairs and which room would be mine. She papered and painted it and brought my bed to the room. There was one problem a giant fly in the ointment of happiness. I was so angry, I didn't know why it was something and it did not take much for my anger to explode all over. I would be in my 30s before I would get help for this devastating situation. I seldom saw mom or my sister and brothers. Judy would tell me when I moved back home at age 18 that she did not even know I was her sister.

Mom would consult her attorney in Lagrange regarding what to do about the situation between my stepfather and I. The attorney told mom that I was lying and making it up. When she told me this many years later I asked her how could a child of 11 ever make up such a story back in the middle of the fifties. I wanted to take that attorney by the neck and shaking until his teeth rattled. Many years later after I was grown up, I found a newspaper clipping in the top drawer of the buffet. It was yellow with age but it was a story of a man with a molested a child. Across the top and mom's handwriting was written, this is where you should be. It took a lot of years to forgive him, but I knew I had to for my own mental health. I still remember, it is clear in my mind as the day went down. We can forgive but we never can forget. Do not think that a sexual predator will ever stop with one child. They can't it's not in their DNA unless they totally and completely surrender to the Lord. Mothers you may think that you can keep an eye on your child while he is around. No mom you can't. He has more ideas in his head, and ways to get around then you can imagine. It took a lot of years but the Lord has healed me in this area, it was one of the many times He carried me.

# Chapter 5

*J* had to change schools when I moved from home to Granddaddy's I had to change schools. I cannot say I was sorry to leave the Shipshewana-Scott school. It's a hard thing to go to school when your teacher doesn't like you, the kids make fun of you because you wear homemade clothes, and you already feel like the scum of the earth because of the abuse. On top of all that, now that I was living with Granddaddy and Mama, I was a PK, also known as a preacher's kid. I was not quite ready for the life of a preacher's kid, where there is always so much scrutiny on what I should have done whether I got it or not.

Before I left Shipshe, I had an accident. Back home, there was this pole with chains hanging down from the top. At the very end of the chains were two bars to hold onto. It was sort of like a maypole, only it was all steel. We would hang onto these bars and swing around on the chains. Sometimes, we would ask someone to give us a push because then we could go higher and faster. We always first dusted our hands with dirt so we wouldn't slip.

This particular day, I guess I hadn't dusted my hands well enough with dirt, and as I was speeding through the air, I realized my hands were slipping. I called out to the girls that were standing on the side to help me, that I was going to fall, but they either didn't hear me or just ignored me. I suddenly found myself flying through the air, and I landed in the worst spot around the pole, a patch of cement and stones. I landed hard and busted my chin, and I still have a tiny stone lodged under my chin.

My wonderful uncles, Mark, Merve, and Meredith, gave me the lovely name of Stony Burk. Stony Burk was a character on a radio program from back then, like The Shadow, Fibber Mcgee and Molly, The Great Gildersleeve, and of course, The Lone Ranger!

I had to go to the doctor for stitches, and not only on the outside of my chin, but also on my tongue, which had been ripped back. The doctor had to secure my tongue back down where it was supposed to be, and he gave me the most horrible tablets to suck on. Those things tasted horrible; so I would stick them in the wastebasket. Only problem was that I put them on top and Mama found them and told Granddaddy. Granddaddy called me in to the study, and his piercing blue eyes told me I had been caught red-handed. He told me how disappointed he was that I would do this. Needless to say prices stopped, and to this day I have never forgotten those piercing blue eyes.

At times I would go out early in the morning when the dew was still on the ground, and I would smell that wonderful smell of the trees and grasses and the leaves. It would smell so much like the lake, oh how I love that smell I missed, I still love to smell that scent. I often wish mom had never sold the cottage at the lake. I loved it there on the farm we had: Linda, a pony, a quarter horse named Ginger I could ride and have more fun on her. At times Mark would take Linda, hitch her up to the cart, and we would write down to see mom and the kids. We were never made to feel very welcome so we never stayed long. My favorite thing was to have Ginger saddled and go for a ride up and down the road. I did this numerous times, this one day I had Ginger saddled and decided to write towards Emmatown riding along nicely when much to my surprise Ginger took off like a shot I'm trying to slow down and she is gold pell-mell for the Emma store, we flew around the corner heading for the church, she finally stopped between the church and a house beside the church. The next thing she

starts bucking, all I could think of was all the stories of cow-
boys who fell off their horse got their foot caught in the stirrup.
I managed to get my feet free of the stirrups, wrapped my
arms around Ginger's neck and swung down off the saddle.
I must've made quite a sight hanging there on Ginger's neck
my feet not quite touching the ground and I'm saying, " Ginger
stop it." To my surprise she looks at me hanging down in front
of her and stopped. I told her to behave herself, swung back
up into the saddle and went home. I never rode out on the
road again I said one time was enough I would stay in the
pastures. I used to ride Ginger and sing. It was a wonderful,
wonderful memory and still is.

The boys always told me not to go up into the attic, I didn't
know why that they were most insistent I could not go up into
the attic. It turns out they had what they called their airplane.
There was a window in the attic they had a chair facing the
window, what looked like a doorframe behind the chair, and a
green blind that they could pull down up or down as to when
they were in their cockpit. I saw the contraption I thought boy is
that dumb but I never told the boys. There were noises coming
out of attic also disturbed me, I would ask the boys about
what that noise was and they always told me it was Uncle
Eli's ghost. I had never seen Uncle Eli, I knew he was old and
dead, but why was he in the attic. It turns out that the so-called
Uncle Eli's ghost was a squirrel, oh my that was something.
The boys used to enjoy telling me the bloody bones story. I
was scared to death to go downstairs in the night. There was
only one bathroom in the house and it was downstairs. What
I was afraid of was that either Uncle Eli's ghost or the bloody
bones would get me. All I can remember of the bloody bones
story is bloody bones on the first step, bloody bones on the
second step. I asked Mark who always told me the story the
most scariest if he remembers the story he said he doesn't
remember, thinks he just might have made it up, but it did a
number on me, so that I would not have to walk the long hall
I had to devise something else to do when I needed the bathroom. The more I thought on it more discouraged I became.

Then I had a brilliant idea, granddaddy's rubbers, so I took one of the rubbers to the room, hid it so no one could see it. Then when I needed to go to the bathroom rather go down the dark hallway I used the rubber, and in the morning poured it out the window. No one was the wiser for a while, but all good things have to come to an end. I was found out and all the uproar I caused, needless to say I again returned to going down the long dark hall, trying to find the light switch at the head of the stairs, and went downstairs. If you don't know what a rubber is instead of having a boot, it's only the bottom part of the boot that makes up the rubber it only comes to your ankles, they are good to use in rainy weather etc.

At night were laying in our beds in in the summer, we had a windows open as we had no AC. We would be able to hear the Amish races down the road to the Emma store, I love to listen to the sounds of the horses running then suddenly one had to slow down, they had reached the Emma Creek Bridge and both could not go over the same time. The Emma store had a wonderful sort of saw all the young Amish man on a Saturday night didn't have anything to do with come to the Emma store and get together just to chat and have a soda. Also in the summer there was many a night I would ride my bike up to the store and bring back a pint of pineapple sherbet for mama and myself. All that tasted s I could ride my bike fast enough that the sherbet to melt I can never see I am sherbet and not think that.

Also in the summer when the other grandchildren came, like Betty's children, we would play games such as Red Rover, Red Rover, gray wolves which had to put play close to dark or was no fun. There was other games we played that I can't recall them. It was also so wonderful when Darrell, Gerald, and Linda came and stayed overnight. We also went out to the pine trees along the property line, there was one limb that was just perfect to put your legs over and hang upside down. Well since I had to wear skirt, it was I see London, I see France, I see Janie's underpants. It was very hard to hang upside down and tuck the skirt under your legs. One night granddaddy and mama had gone away. Darrell and I were alone in the house. We had gone to bed early just to be safe. When all of a sudden we heard someone trying to get in the front door. Mama always kept that door locked so it was a surprise that someone would try the front door. All of a sudden our little rat terrier Penny came flying from nowhere barking up a storm, Darrell and I were praying just scared to pieces, when suddenly whoever he was left. That night Darrell and I felt like God used Penny to save us and carry us through a various frightening moment.

One morning I got up went downstairs and found everybody so excited in the kitchen, all three of the boys couldn't wait till I would go and look down in the cellar. So I did and what I saw was totally alien to me there were little black things running around in the basement I turned around and asked what. All the boys and mama started to laugh. A ewe had delivered twins which is unusual for sheep, and she rejected the twins. So calls were made to granddaddy's to ask if they would take the lambs, and they said yes. I always thought all lambs were born white, but these were born black. They were so cute, they were named Kate and Duplakate, and we changed his name to Doopie. It was my job to go out and feed them after they got off the bottle, to feed them their grain. We had them in the chicken coop area that was fenced in, and had the chicken house on. Though it was shelter for the lambs as well as the chickens or should I say Banties. Katie had this one thing she loved to do, she would get a running start from across the yard as I was leaving, running full speed she loved to slam into my back, so I got smart and put a pail there so when she hit me the pail took the biggest hit and I could escape fairly unharmed.

I really loved granddaddy's one thing he insisted on every morning, family worship. Now I admit that at first I thought it was the dumbest thing this side of heaven. As I have gotten older I have so appreciated the times of family worship, and the fact that granddaddy and mama loved me enough to not let me have my own way but come to family worship. I would not be the prayer warrior I am today had I not had that wonderful upbringing that you pray about everything. Now some people think that, Papa God is sitting up in his heaven with this giant two by four ready to hit you one upside the head. That is not the God I know. I thought that at one time too. But I have found He is a most loving God, and at times when I feel so down I can tell Him, I just need to crawl up in your lap and have you hold me. And I can feel myself sitting in His lap holding and comforting me.

# Chapter 6

$\mathcal{S}$ince I moved across the road I was in the Topeka school district. Now Emma is 5 miles from Topeka, and 5 miles from Shipshewana. The dividing line for the two districts went right down the center of the room. I remember when they paved that road it was so exciting we had the threshers so we had to fix a meal. All the neighbors gathered together and helped the person who had to get the meal. There was a large number of men who would come to thrash the wheat and the oats and we had to feed them. But it was so funny mama needed something from the store and it was hard to get up there because they had blacktop going down the middle of the road so she drove on the only side she could. After thrashing was over they had a big meeting when the houses settle up as they called it, but it was so neat because we had homemade ice cream oh was that good! My mouth still waters thinking of that good ice cream. And naturally all of us children had more fun playing with the neighbor kids.

My first day at Honeyville was not bad at all. I was one of four non-Amish students. Most of the children when they came to first grade only spoke Pennsylvania Dutch. So they had to learn English and they were wonderful teachers and took the time the children needed. Our class was the class of 57 what a class we were. It was nothing like Shipshewana., And I was so glad to be going there. I was thinking of writing this book and planning on it I had one of the girls from the class tell me she too had transferred in. That she had hated her old school too. I was so glad to learn I wasn't the only one. The kids were wonderful they tried to teach me Dutch of which most of it I have forgotten sad to say. But there are times when I'll hear somebody talking and I'll catch a few phrases that I know what they're saying and that is always a joy to me. I will always cherish my time at Honeyville what a wonderful class of 57. In fact we still get together for reunions in May and October. Whenever we had a fire drill I was scared to death. We had these huge tubes that went down the side of the building. I am petrified of heights, and slides that are high. All the boys loved going down the tube, but we girls did not like going down. We had to tuck our skirts under our legs or the air was blowing dresses up into a balloon which the boys would love. As I got to know my classmates better I kind of liked one of the English boys. But I kept looking and thinking of a certain Amish boy who I thought was everything. Problem was he was Amish, and there was no way in God's green earth I would ever turn Amish. Sure is fun to get in the buggy and ride in the summertime not the winter. When we were in eighth grade we did a play, there was a part that someone had to be the Princess so I was picked as the Princess I had a cardboard with stars on it. I don't recall the name of the play, it was the second play that I was in while in school at Honeyville. I thoroughly enjoyed acting I loved it so much so that when we did the school prophecy I told him that I was going to go to Hollywood and be a movie star. Needless to say I have never made it. They took us on a trip to see the Science and Industry Museum in Chicago. It was a wonderful trip!! I sat on the bus with the guy I liked that was English and we had fun. They talked me into going up the escalator, but they also had been talking about someone getting their foot caught at the top and being drug underneath the escalator. I knew it was impossible because it was too tiny. Needless to say as I got to the top my toe caught and I tripped. I have been petrified of escalators ever since. Even going to Honduras as a medical missionary I had to board a plane in Miami unbeknownst to me all they had was escalators going to the plane.

I asked him if there wasn't an elevator and they said no. What they did was turn off the escalator and let me walk up but I was positive that thing would take off any second while I was on it. I was so glad to find Houston instead of Miami

After graduation from high school I was at home preparing to go to nursing school in Fort Wayne, when a young tall handsome young man knocked on the door. It was the guy I had a crush on, he was still Amish I told him I was going to nursing school. It never entered my head to tell him to write to me and give him my address or get his! I was so thrilled that he had come to see me. I still don't know how he found me, because I was no longer at granddaddy's. Mama and I had a big fight and it was the struggle that broke the camel's back. She could take no more of my anger and my blowups. How that dear lady put up with me I don't know. But she did from age 11 to 18. One time I was supposed to wash the dishes, only I had other plans I ran back to the barn into the cornfield thinking no one could find me. It wasn't long until I realized that Mark was right behind and he grabbed me by the scruff of the neck and said you get in that house and you do those dishes so I did. I was not a happy camper but who cared. And the dishes got washed and Mama got to sit down and rest a bit.

Mama was quite ill with diabetes and she had also had a bout with cancer. She also had arthritis which flared up sometimes and made it difficult to play the piano plus other things that you use your hands for and the pain was so great she didn't want to do it. I did not understand that until I got arthritis. From the time I moved in and the newness wore off I thought Mama was faking it. And I made the mistake of saying that one time in granddaddy's hearing. Those blue eyes pierced and flashed to no end as he firmly informed me in no uncertain terms I had better never speak to or of his wife like that again. Needless to say I didn't. But after I left and have had have the time to reflect, I put her through pure hell. If I could've had the counseling I desperately needed it would have been different, but Mama loved me in spite of my anger, and she prayed for me. When she died granddaddy was at her bedside, I was staying at Mark's house in Indianapolis when the call came in. Granddaddy told Mark that he had promised Mama that we would all meet her in heaven. Boy did those words haunt me many, many times. I am so thankful for those prayers and even though she's gone and he's gone I have looked towards heaven and told them I was so sorry for what I put them through.

# Chapter 7

*I*t was hard to leave Honeyville, I so loved my fellow students, we had become like a little family. They didn't care that I wore homemade clothes because their mom's also made homemade clothes for them. At graduation night we were all sad that we were leaving, for the Amish kids they would see each other in church or family gatherings and things that were happening in their district. For us English kids it was a totally different ballgame. We were going on to high school and that meant changing schools. Since granddaddy was on the board of the new Christian high school called Bethany, I had to go to Bethany. I did not want to go to Bethany I wanted to go on to Topeka high school. But that was not a possibility for a PK and a board member. So for three years I went to Bethany I did not like it I wanted out of there so bad I could taste it, and that only fueled my already raging anger even more. We had to drive there and Ivan's kids had to go also, so the three of us drove to Bethany every day. After I moved back home when I got so upset with Mama about something which I have no recollection what it was, Mama said that she had had it. I fully understand her reasoning, for seven years she had taken my anger outbursts, and she could take no more. There was one thing Mama did for me though on my 16th birthday they threw a wonderful surprise party for me and all my friends from church. It was the most awesome birthday party I had ever had I can still see all the girls sitting there in the living room in a circle. We had a wonderful time and I so enjoyed it. Thinking back I have to remember different things that happened as we girls got together in our teenage years. We'd go to each other's houses and have a slumber party which always included a pillow fight. Sometimes we'd go home with each other after church then come back to church and go home. I'll never forget one day when I went home with Janie and we went to the barn see the cows, just walking around. We entered the barn and there's this one cow penned up; as we looked at her we noticed something very strange about this cow. We saw baby calf standing close, but there was something coming out of her butt!! We both made a mad dash to the house, flew into the living room where her parents had company and promptly told them that there was something wrong with the cow, that in the back her guts were falling out! We could not understand why nobody was upset, it didn't make sense that this cow's guts were falling out at least that's what we thought. We could tell her parents were embarrassed of the way we were talking and they just told us to go upstairs and forget about it, so we did. I don't know when I learned that the guts were falling out of a cow she was just passing her placenta. But I'll never forget that day and Janie's house.

When I moved back home I had to live with my stepdad again. Mother did not leave him so I had to deal with him. I was still very, very angry and every time I looked at that man, I hated him. You might say with a purple passion I hated. He tried to tell me what to do and each time I would tell him in no uncertain terms, very angry voice he was not my father and I didn't have to do what he said. He would usually just turn around and walk out to the barn which pleased me as he was out of the house. I remember one time in particular after I had come back from the senior trip to New Orleans, and Biloxi Mississippi. I had bought a friendship ring and I wore it, I usually took it off before I got into the house, but this one day I forgot and he saw it. And he started to let me have it, needless to say I took the ring off and let him have it. We thoroughly enjoyed our senior trip and I had started wearing shorts but I couldn't wear them around the house, so I put them on and wore a skirt over them. Then when I was away from the house I took the skirt off. It worked pretty well.

I loved my senior year at Shipshewana! We had a wonderful time! Living in Indiana basketball season was all and is all the rage. Our team one was one of those two teams in the sectionals. We were playing Elkhart, we usually never beat Elkhart but we had a great team this time. The guys were scheduled to play in the midafternoon, we wanted to have time off to attend the game. But our principal who we had named the Beanie Brown, as he was such a nerd, decided in his infinite wisdom that no one could go to the game. The guys had to go on their own. We were all furious, the whole senior class. But the cheerleaders and I decided to ignore the mandate, we were going to go support our team, as we had never gotten that far before. We were County Champs and this could not go without someone being there to support the team. When we came back Beanie Brown threatened to have us all expelled from school for a day or two, we thought it was worth it. He never did carry through on his threat and we had supported our boys that day.

For graduation we decided we wanted to look like New Orleans. So we decorated with glitter all over the stage and made it look as much like New Orleans as we possibly could, it was beautiful. We had our 50th reunion and there were those same orchids again. We had a wonderful time getting together and see how everybody looked after 50 years. We had changed yet most of us looked the same and it was a wonderful evening of pizza, friendship, and catching up on everything.

As we all know when you're in your senior year you are supposed to make the decision as to what you are going to do for the rest of your life. I wanted to be a beautician in the worst way, I had been getting my hair done for a while, and I really liked what I saw, it really intrigued me. But mother had other ideas I had to be a nurse, I did not want to be a nurse pure and simple. But with my mother she had a way of wearing you down and you just did it to shut her up. So the plans were made for me to be a nurse. And I was a very unhappy camper. I would not find out for many years why she insisted I be a nurse. It turns out when she was little and at the orphan's home she would go under the shade tree that was close to the building and play nurse. She told me if she had known how beautician work would gain so much speed and have such a need, she would've agreed. So for 47 years I was a nurse and I tried my best to get out of it numerous times to no avail. I had to retire to get away from nursing.

It was close to time for graduation, mom had taken me to Shipshewana to get my hair done. I was so glad because with all of the home perms, my hair was like a straw stack, it was stiff it had need to be trimmed and it was a royal mess. So I had my hair cut and got a new perm. As with all new perms it pulled my hair up a little higher than it normally would but it relaxed a little bit in a week or two. I got my senior pictures taken and I thought my hairdo looked wonderful. One night there was a knock on the door, mom and I looked at each other wondering who was coming at this hour. It was close to suppertime and the men hadn't come in from the barn yet. So mom opened the door and there to our surprise stood one of the pastors of the Church, and Orvan. Ivan looked like he would rather be anyplace other than their house. Orvan took over and proceeded to tell me that I need to get in front of the church, tell them I was sorry for cutting my hair and all would be okay, I could remain a member of the Emma Mennonite church. I couldn't stand Orvan, how he got to be an associate pastor of was beyond my understanding. I knew this man a bit too well more than most people because I was a PK. Orvan's wife Grace was mom's best friend. She had diabetes, severe diabetes and this man refused to purchase her insulin for her, she was a housewife and the only way she had of making money for her insulin was giving piano lessons. We girls used to get quite tickled at Orvan. He always walked around looking like he had been dipped in a barrel of dill pickle juice. As you well know dill pickle juice is quite sour. I never saw the man smile, I really don't think it was in his DNA. There were times when we were a prayer meeting when us girls knew that one of the older ladies in the church would be popping her head up and checking out who was there and who wasn't. And Orvan would be popping his head up glaring at us girls every time. Well the problem was the more he glared the more we girls got tickled in which we had a difficult time suppressing our laughter. This would only make him glare even more which only made us more tickled. The interesting thing was we never got called down on our getting so tickled.

# Chapter 8

The day came much too rapidly for me to go to Fort Wayne to nursing school. I dreaded it with every fiber of my being but I had to go, I didn't have a choice. Mom had found an older lady for me to live with. She had a beautiful house on Forest Park Boulevard. Now back in the day Forest Park Boulevard was one of the places that the wealthy went and built their homes, so there are a lot of large older homes on that street even to this day. She showed me to my room which was very nice, better than what I had at home. I thought everything was going along nicely and then she started treating me like a child, killing me when I needed to study. How would I study in all this rot? I did not like that and I told her in no uncertain terms I wasn't a kid anymore. I knew I had to study and how much I needed to study and I didn't need her to tell me how to. She didn't like it very well but I thought oh well whatever. We did our first four months in Forest Park School. We had several rooms in the basement that we used. (My grandchildren went there for their grade school I thought that was rather interesting). We learned how to make a bed, how to take the temperature, how to give a bath properly, how to make a bed with the patient in it how to be patient when the patient was not in the bed. Then we also had nutrition and some other things that I don't remember anymore. I had learned over the grapevine that when it came time to divide up into the three hospitals if the administrator knew that you definitely did not want to go to a certain hospital, she would make sure you went there. So I made it well know that I didn't want to go to Lutheran Hospital. In the end I got to go to Lutheran Hospital. I had seen the Lutheran grads and I felt they had the best training out of all three hospitals in Fort Wayne. I had wonderful instructor! She was fun and made the whole learning process not bad. I'll never forget the first day we had to give a bath to a patient in bed. We all crowded around the bed and we looked at our patient who was more there than here. The biggest problem was it was a man. We did not mind washing his torso and his legs, but to wash his private parts that was more than many of us could swallow. But we knew we had to do it we had to learn. At last one brave soul went for the gusto. The gentleman got bathed clean, and we girls walked out of the room where we were met by our instructor. We told her we did not like the idea of bathing a man, but she said that that was part of nursing, still to the embarrassment of us all. But we grew to deal with it and I think don't about it anymore. it was just part of the routine that we had to perform, but it still is an interesting memory from my days as a student nurse.

Another time my instructor wanted me to give a shot to a patient. Again the patient was pretty much not with it. So I gave the shot and the next day my instructor came to me and told me the patient had died. I asked her in horror if I killed the patient. She laughed and said no the patient was almost ready to go anyhow, it just was that person's time.

Then came my time to put in a catheter. My instructor had found this little lady to do this with. She really didn't know what was going on, bless her heart. She was always muttering something, so I went ahead and did a great job my instructor was very pleased so was I. There was one student in our class that I dearly loved. Her name was Yvone. She was a beautiful young black woman and could she dance. She had the smoothest moves you ever saw. She was like a sister to me, she would tell me stuff I wouldn't take up with anybody else white or black. When we graduated from nursing school I lost track of my friend Yvone. I have wished over the years I knew where she was so I could go see her. I did see her once when she invited me to her house and I got to see her baby. He was so cute. I just leaned over to pick him up and snuggled him, such a little doll!

One day I walked into the room and for once we had a young patient whose name was Bill. I struck up a conversation with him for the longest time. I really enjoyed talking to him, he was interesting and funny a breath of fresh air in the hospital. When Bill was released from the hospital, we started to date. He had A 1957 Chevy teal and white and it was his pride and joy. I had left the house with the lady that wanted to treat me like a kid, and three of us nursing students got together and rented an apartment. It was an upstairs apartment and it was really nice. I really enjoyed living there. One night Bill came up and we were sitting on the couch talking when all of a sudden he reached up and turned the light on and off. I thought okay this is interesting. I was still thinking about that when he asked me to marry him and of course I said yes. Why wouldn't I say yes to the guy that loves me, and wants to marry me? As he left that night the snow had started up all softly. As he got down to step off the curb, he turned around and looked back up at the window where I was standing and waved at me. I have never forgotten that scene, it was always special to me. So then I had to buy a graduation gown from nursing school as well as plan a wedding shortly after school. I graduated in June from nursing school, and we would be married on 25 August 1962. Since mom was not close by, Ruth helped me with a lot of the details, I wanted to carry pink roses and Bill had other ideas. Had it not been for his aunt Ruth I think I would've given in just to please him. Mom came down and helped me find my dress. Then the hoops were all one style so my dress was interesting trying to walk and see things but it did look beautiful. It had pearls and sequins and a sweetheart neckline of lace in the bodice. At the waist there was a bow. I forget which you call the over skirt and under skirt of the gown, but on the over skirt it was split up the center and there was lace all the way around the edge, it was beautiful. I felt like a princess in that dress. Bill chose the cake, which was an arrangement I'd never seen before or since. It had bottom layers and then they started tiering up on both sides. I'm still not sure how it was but anyway it was a pretty cake and it was one thing I didn't have to think about. My girls were all dressed alike in beautiful pink gowns and cabbage roses for their heads. There was a total of 17 in the party. I thought I would never find enough girls for the wedding party.

# Chapter 9

$\mathcal{G}$raduation was over and I was working at the hospital. I made a $1.62 hour as a new graduate nurse. I had to take the bus to get to Fairfield where the hospital was. One day I was asked if I would mind moving up to sixth floor, it was a brand-new unit and they felt that I would be an asset to the floor. It was there I met Mrs. Rehm, she was the head nurse, an old Army nurse, who was not afraid to get her hands dirty. If someone needed to be turned over, a bed pan was given to them by her. She also assisted in cleaning out isolation when we had one. She was like no other nurse I knew. I decided that if I had to be a nurse I wanted to be like her. I had a lot of respect for her. Her work was over and above the call of duty for RN.

One day we had a man in the hospital who had what we call a TURP. He had a catheter in and had normal saline flowing in one way and coming out the catheter. This little man decided he had had enough of the hospital that he was going home. All of a sudden we discovered he was missing so we went on a search. He was found outside the hospital walking down the sidewalk the back of his gown flopping in the breezes, pieces of his catheter on the bushes. We collected them as fast as we could and brought him back to the room totally amazed that he was able to do this without any pain.

I shall never forget my first heart attack. I was a fresh grad and I saw the call light on, I went into the room and this man was sitting up red-faced gasping for air and holding his chest.

There was no doubting this man was in trouble. I had no clue as to what to do but he needed somebody fast. I shot out the door and happened to see his doctor on the floor so I called him and Mrs. Reagan and in seconds we were all back in the room. We grabbed an oxygen tank and were giving the gentleman oxygen. The doctor tried his best to get the medication to relieve the pain and stop everything was happening. It so shook me up, and I could hardly keep going making my rounds. I learned a lot that first year. I'm so thankful for the hospital and the training they give me back then. I do not believe that I could have done all the things I have done for my life in nursing if it hadn't been for that wonderful training they gave me. Sometimes I hated, it some days it wasn't bad but I really did not want to be a nurse but I thought I would be the best I could be.

The day for our wedding came up. It was a beautiful day sun shining just a perfect August day for a wedding. I got my dress on and Ruth helped my mom come back for a while. We took pictures as you usually do. The bridesmaids walked down the aisle, they looked beautiful in their pink dresses. There was a sash that was part of the dress that was a deeper pink. As they lined up and I saw Bills white dinner jacket and all of the guys, Uncle Bill and I stepped into the entrance of the sanctuary. Mercy that is one long isle going down to the altar. As I stood there with Uncle Bill, all of a sudden I got so scared I didn't know if I wanted to run or walk down that aisle. I seriously thought about turning around and running, but why I have no clue. I looked at Bill he was fun to be with yet sometimes caused intense pain in the touch, but overall not a bad guy, especially when you compare him to me, a girl so with much baggage, it is a miracle that he wanted to marry me. I had not yet come to the place I could tell anyone about my secret. In my mixed up mind I thought the only way that a man could love you was to have sex. Someone that has been abused will either totally shun anything to do with making love, or they may become very promiscuous. Some even are so horrified at what has happened they have blocked out every memory and when something happens to trigger that memory they go ballistic. There is no memory whatsoever of the incident. They have all the symptoms of the anger and the outbursts but they don't know why. This secret I kept from Bill everyday right to now. I do not believe he and I would've ended up in divorce if I had told him. Granted he had a hard time leaving the single life, he loved people going out with people partying and I was a stay-at-home girl and working. I finally got to the point and I know now that I was in this situation that you call I will reject you before you can reject me. It is not fun being in this mode and I was in it for a number of years until I got the free when I was in my 30s. It wasn't all Bill's fault, I know that and for many years I was so hoping to be with him but it was not to be. He just couldn't do it for some reason. I think of him often and I pray for him that's the best I can do.

# Chapter 10

$\mathscr{I}$t was so hard going through the divorce and leaving Bill, I thought we would be married forever. One thing happened during our marriage that was really devastating. Unbeknownst to me I had a birth defect because my uterus was what they called a bicornate uterus. Which means instead of the pear-shaped mine went off into two forms on each side. The result was when I would get pregnant I would lose the child usually in the first trimester. I was in the process of losing my first child when Bill was at work, I called him to come home I was freaking out. We lived in what you call a shotgun house, which means its one room after another in succession of the length of the house. I couldn't get up in my bedroom to go to the bathroom, as I was in so much pain. But Bill never came home that night and it hurt me beyond words. So this was what I was thinking about as we proceeded with the divorce. I kept working at Lutheran it was a good job and was getting some good money. I stayed in our apartment for some time. One day I noticed my headlight was out. I had stopped for gas and the station owner told me to come back later and he would fix my headlight. Sounded good to me, so I took my car to the station in the evening and I noticed a guy leaning on a stack of tires. He wasn't bad looking had pretty blue eyes and blonde hair. I got out of my car, and went into the station. The guy asked me what I needed, and I told him the owner said I should come back in the evening and he would fix my headlight. He said he could do it so I said okay. While he was changing my headlight we got to talking, and I thought he was pretty interesting. He had two kids from a previous marriage, and he had custody of them. That didn't bother me, I love kids. One thing led to another and we begin dating exclusively. After time he asked me to marry him and I said yes. Little did I know that this man was abusive. He hid it well, to see him and talk to him you would never guess. Dick and I were married a total of seven years, in that time I had more miscarriages. I had no idea what was wrong.

I went to the gynecologist and he decided to run some tests that was when I found out about the bicornate uterus which he promptly went into surgery for. The doctor went in and took out half of my uterus and sewed it back together, then he told me to go get pregnant. Up to this point I had lost five babies which is not any fun I can tell you. I promptly got pregnant and in the process of losing the child I was told that he was not yet six months in pregnancy, in the state of Indiana to bury a baby he/she must be at six months.

As time went on the beatings were worse. One time we were in the car driving around the curves of Shore Lake and he threatened to crash the car into a tree. I was scared to death. All I could think of was in killing us both what would happen to the children. I really loved those kids as my own. Another time we were driving down the road and he was beating me with one hand as he guided the car with the other so I decided to slug him back and I did. At this point I did not love the man. But I was concerned about Lisa and Dan. Because if I left he would be on them instead of me. I would learn later that he had come from an abusive home.

After I had delivered my sixth child, I soon learned I was pregnant again. I went back to the doctor for an exam, he told me my last pregnancy I had been six months along. I was devastated that I had not given my child a burial because I had been told that the baby wasn't at six months. As I talked to the doctor I told him that I wanted my tubes tied, that I could not go through another pregnancy. He told me in no uncertain terms that he wasn't giving up after all his work, and if I thought he would go straight to he double hockey sticks. Needless to say I went back home to Howe weeping. My family doctor did not want to take over the care of me, so he called and spoke with a doctor in Elkhart. Because I had a blood clot in my leg they put me on heparin which thins the blood and you have to check the blood frequently so you know your blood is not too thin.

On May 5, 1970 I started with horrible pain in my belly. The pain would just not go away. It was one consistent pain. So I asked my neighbor Andy down the street to take me to the doctors. They put me in the examining room and Dr. Maddox came in and checked me, not saying anything, he was just very solemn. As he opened the door of the room he turned to me and said that he would like Dr. Reed to look at me. I looked at him and said my uterus is rupturing isn't it. He looked so shocked, and said yes I think so but I want Reed's opinion to. Dr. Reed was the surgeon of the office so he came in and examined me, and immediately sent me to the hospital. Andy had her little one-year-old baby with this us as we rushed from Howe to Lagrange to the hospital. It was about 5 miles away. I was thinking if I had not changed doctors and I was having to make a trip to Elkhart I probably would've died on the way, because I was told to continue the heparin the whole pregnancy. My doctors in Howe stopped the heparin. At the hospital they took x-rays then sent be back to the room to wait it seemed like forever until doctors got there. They rushed me into surgery and delivered my precious Renée, she was five weeks early, weighing 3 ½ pounds. She had curly hair but I couldn't see her right away. However, as they brought me out from the recovery room I was able to look around and see that she was clear back in the corner of the nursery on rocking band. I don't know why it didn't sink in she's on rocking bed that means trouble but it didn't.

During the whole pregnancy Dick was telling me he hoped I'd lose the baby. I tried my best to ignore him but the words hurt so badly. 3 ½ hours after surgery he finally came in to the room and told me she was dead. I didn't say anything, if I would have opened my mouth I'm not sure what would have come out. Dr. Maddox walked into the room and asked Dick if he had told me yet and he said yes. He would later tell me that when he told me about the death of my baby that I screamed. I told him if I had screamed Dr. Maddox would've heard. I wanted to have my baby buried with my daddy at Violet Cemetery in Goshen. But Dick came back and said someone had said we couldn't do it. Later I would find out that she could have been buried at the head or feet of my daddy. The pastor said that the church had cemetery plots in Lagrange Cemetery. The wife of a pastor had died in childbirth along with her child, so the church bought these plots for the church's use. The only other people buried in that site besides Renée, is another little girl about the same age.

Within six months I looked like I was pregnant again and I want to see Dr. Reed Taylor because I was dissatisfied with Maddox. He insisted on repairing the uterus instead of removing it, and now I was in another fix. Dr. Taylor wanted me to go see a gynecologist, and he examined me in the emergency room where he had better light. Dick was there and all at once he blew up and he ranted and raved and carried on like a madman and Dr. Taylor just sat there and let him talk. Dr. Taylor told me that if that was what I was living with no wonder my nerves were where they were. I ended up going to see a gynecologist that my doctor recommended in Goshen and he took me to surgery and did a total hysterectomy. Then I got an infection so I had to stay longer in the hospital finally I was able to go home but with specific instructions not to have any form of sex until I had my six week checkup. Dick had other ideas and I told him we could not do this, which it was dangerous for me, but that didn't matter, he raped me. As a result I had a huge hematoma which was a blood clot in the upper part of where they had done surgery. I almost had to go back to surgery to get that taken care of.

We decided to go to marriage counseling to try and save our marriage. After a number of visits the counselor took me aside and said, " Jane, you need to get out and get out fast your life is at stake. That scared me about kids, if I wasn't there to take the brunt of the abuse what would happen to Lisa and Danny? Well I finally came up with an idea. I told Dick that the marriage was over and I was going to get custody of the children. I knew I didn't have a snowball's chance in July, but it worked. The divorce was finalized and he gave custody of the children to their natural mother. Unbeknownst to me she had moved in shortly before Christmas and on

Christmas Eve she was in a car wreck and was stranded with the children. She finally got home and he was so angry he threw her to the floor and began to beat the back of her head on the metal wedge between the parquet floor and carpeting. He broke a lot of vessels in the back of her head so that she has to continue to take medication for the rest of her life to keep the vessels open. Lisa and Danny pulled Dick off their mom, which was the only thing that saved her life. She called to Fort Wayne and family came up and rescued her and the kids. I was so happy that she had custody I could hardly contain myself.

# Chapter 11

*I* decided to leave the area and Mark and Phyllis were living in Indianapolis, they had moved there from there from Emmatown so their daughter Robin could go to blind school. I looked for work and found it at Marion County General hospital, which we know today as Wishard. I worked in the ER which was very exciting. When I began to work at MCGH I was fascinated to see how the ER worked. Since M CGH was a county hospital, all inmates in the county that needed medical treatment were sent to us. They even had jail cells where they could house people for longer periods of time and receive their medical treatment. There are number things I did not know when I first began to work in the ER. So I was put in triage to see how I would do. One day I was supposed to give this gentleman a shot, he needed penicillin. He was high on something and as I went to getting the shots, all of a sudden he had me pinned against the walls. I was alone in the room and I was doing my best to talk him down. The RN on duty and the doctor heard the commotion in the room, they rushed in and it took both of them to rescue me from this gentleman. Needless to say he still got a shot and it was a huge needle and I never enjoyed giving a shot so much in my life.

They also taught me how to draw blood, the RN who was with me slowly guided me in how to draw blood. I was so shocked when I hit the vein I about fell over. I have been drawing blood for many years since that time. Once I got used to triage, I was put in the ER. I found it so fascinating.

You never knew what was coming. One day I was working with one of the residents and I had a man with his head split open. He was drunk and very uncooperative. Here I am with a straight razor trying to shave this dude's head and he's wiggling around and carrying on about his friends and that I don't make another dent in his head. Finally the resident across the room was coming in to suture after I got it cleaned up. He never missed a stitch and in no uncertain terms told that drunk he better straighten up. Needless to say I was able to complete my job without any more problems thanks to the doctor I was working with.

Another time we had a man that overdosed he was flailing arms and legs and trying to come off that gurney and it took all of us, I think there were at least eight of us trying to hold him down so Dr. Gilkey could administer a Narcan infusion. Within seconds after the infusion he was awake, cussing up a storm. One of the residents looked at him and told him in no uncertain terms that he should thank Dr. Gilkey because he had just saved his life. Not too long ago I was taken to the ER at Wishard. All of a sudden I heard someone call for Dr. Gilkey. I got so excited I think you mean he is still there? Sure enough there was Dr. Gilkey he still looked the same hadn't changed a bit maybe someday I'll get to thank him for what he taught me in the ER, I loved that Doc. All the Doc's were so great to answer questions, give us

instructions everything to help nurses in the down times. Sometimes they would help us learn hands-on. I loved my time at Wishard.

There're two incidences that I will share with you one about the kid was brought in with a hand injury in a fire truck. They came roaring into the ER Bay, yelling something that most of us couldn't understand. The firemen explained that they had a call to pick up a severe hand injury. They had not taken off the glove for fear of damaging the hand more than it was already. We got the girl into the ER, the doctors removed the glove, and it was a very minor injury. We all just shook our heads that all this fuss was made, and that the fire truck had been taken out of service for this injury.

I think the one situation that got to me the most was when a very small baby guesstimate under a year, was brought into the ER. She was about a year old. She was a beautiful black child. She had gorgeous long eyelashes. This was the first time that I had seen a black child with bruises. In Lagrange County Black folk were nonexistent where I grew up. They would only be seen in Elkhart, as Goshen was very racial. I never could figure out **why** people were prejudiced, I still can't. I overheard the doctors talking about the child. As the mother stood outside of the room putting on a show. She would fall in squalid carry-on, when no one showed up she peeked out around the side of the area where she was at to see if anyone was coming. I just happened upon her from the opposite direction as I saw her start over and over and over. The doctors said the judge sent the child home with the mother with the promise that if the child stop breathing again she would not have custody. The doctors did what they could for the baby, she was transported up to pediatrics, where she would eventually die. Needless to say that put quite a damper on the ER staff.

One day I was walking to the holding room, which held all the inmates on gurneys, and they were handcuffed to the gurney. Before I could get to the room, I ran into one of our Pinkerton security guards. Oh my, I was smitten the moment I saw him. We chatted a little bit, then I needed to go into the holding room and take care of the need. The guard's name was Steve and a chance encounter turned into much more over the months. I got the assignment that I needed to go into the jail area to check out an inmate that was in one of the holding cells I thought okay no problem. I expected the officer that was there that let me in to go with me, he didn't. So I stepped into the first set of bars they closed the door. That feeling you get when you hear that first clang of the metal bars and door closing behind you, gives you the creepiest feeling. Almost scared, I was led into the next section and again the door clanged behind me. The officer pointed me to the cell and unlocked it, I peered in, as he turned and left me. Now I was even more concerned, it was a long dark cell and at the far end of the cell was a black man that I could hardly make out. He was a perfect gentleman I don't know why he was put in there. I got his vitals and the information I needed and hollered for the officer to come and let me out. He did acting as if it was the drudgery work of the week to do that for me. Needless to say I was not very impressed with the officer.

Stephen and I began to date on a regular basis. His best buddy Art was into racecars, also known as thunder cars. Steve helped Art work on the racecar. Essentially building from scratch. And I found it so interesting as I watched them, at one time had seriously considered being a motorcycle mechanic. So this was just right up my alley. After a number of months Stephen and I got married. I was so happy I just loved that man to no end. We had so much fun together, and we so enjoyed each other's company. But one day still dragging my baggage, I went over to where Stephen was working on the race car. I didn't say anything but later there was a break in the conversation of the guys, then I called to Steve but before telling what I wanted to say, he turned around and made an rather nasty remark to me. He had never spoken to me before like that. I was hurt to the core, and also very angry. I didn't say a word I just turned and walked away, got in the car drove home, called Mark and asked them to come and help me move. I have wished 100 times if I have wished it once, that he had told me to wait a couple days so I cooled off and then make a decision. I was on the road when Steve caught up with me. He wanted me to pull over but I was still fuming and I didn't. Later he would tell me that he came home to tell me that he was sorry, and found me gone. I have regretted this action ever since it occurred. I would come up from Florida and see Steve begging him to come back to Florida with me. But he always refused, and he never asked me to come back up to Indianapolis. I would come have back in a flash if he had asked. I have never forgotten him. He was as a lot of people say my soul mate. It is amazing what you do when you are so mixed up and you have all his anger built up and there's no way to release it and get it out of your life. I'm sure some of you reading this book know what I am talking about. I still think of it to this day, but now my biggest concern is that the Lord would save him. You may ask if I didn't love Bill and Dick, yes but not like I did Steve. He was an excellent husband you couldn't ask for a better. I got my divorce but I was not happy. It was not long after that I moved to Florida Tarpon Springs.

# Chapter 12

*I* decided to leave Indianapolis, and moved to Florida because Lisa and Danny's mother felt I was interfering with her raising the children. I had a nurse's aide who had moved to Florida and told me to come down. So I did, I moved to Tarpon Springs. I loved it there, on New Year's Day of 1974 I was swimming in the Gulf. I was told that a year from then I would not be swimming on New Year's Day. I laughed at them when they told me that but come New Year's Day 1975 I didn't go swimming. It was too cold, and it thinned my blood.

I was renting a 10 x 8 travel trailer. I used to laugh and say that I could get out of bed and fall into the bathroom. When I took a shower I had to fight with the shower curtain because it was so tiny. But it was a roof over my head and it was okay. I got work at Tarpon Springs Convalescent Center. I was the evening charge nurse on one of the wings. The other RN who was on duty with me had no clue what to do, so she depended on me to help her out a lot which I did not mind. One of the guys that worked at the center, kept asking me to go to church. I wasn't interested and I told him so. I was dating a guy whose last name was Clock, his nickname was Tick Tock. We would go to the Moose club, and go out on the gulf quite a bit on his boat. I just love being on the water. Well one day Tick Tock's almost ex-wife appeared on the scene. She stayed overnight and I was furious. He'd been telling me all along that they were getting a divorce. Well my wonderful car had died so I couldn't go anywhere, then I remembered that this guy from work could pick me up and take me to church. What had I to lose, it was better than sitting around thinking about what's going on at the other end of the park. I got dressed up like you did for Lutheran Church. I was told later that I would like a scared little more coming into the church that day. There was a hippie looking guy sitting in the front playing guitar and singing. The pastor got up and he wasn't dressed up either. So I'm looking around wondering what on earth is going on. Well there was a strange guy named Carl who kept going around saying how excited he was to go to church, personally I thought he was nuts. I for the life of me could not figure out how anybody in their right mind would be excited about going to church. I had gone because when I was a kid I had to. While I was at home with mom and my stepdad, I'd go to church Sunday morning, Sunday evening, and usually didn't make it on Wednesday because of the farm.

But when I moved up to granddaddy's we went Sunday morning, Sunday evening, Wednesday evening, Bible school, Sunday school, revival meetings like the one that my uncle Andy preached when I was age 9. He scared us with hellfire and brimstone messages so that all of us young girls decided better for hands up for salvation otherwise we were doomed. So we did, it did not matter we did not really understand, we went to the classes they had, we got baptized. And we were told we were saved and baptized and going to heaven. OK one big problem there, I knew about Jesus, I did not know Him as a personal friend, Savior, or someone who would come to my side and carry me if I needed Him.

I kept watching everyone, there was something different about them, not that they weren't dressed up like you did when you went to Lutheran Church. You could see it in the faces, even in their singing. And I got to wanting what I saw. But I was afraid to ask anybody about it, so I just kept watching. They talked about being baptized in the Holy Ghost, I did not want anything to do with the Holy Ghost. I thought it was not for us it was only for the disciples. But I finally decided to tell God well if you want me to have this Holy Ghost I'm open to it. But

I definitely did not want what they called speaking in tongues. One day a friend of mine Cathy and her fiancé Bill asked me to go with them to Bradenton to a Christian retreat, to hear the group Revelation. Cathy was unable to go due to her mother not feeling well. But she insisted that Bill and I go down. On the way down Bill started talking to me about accepting gifts. He asked me if I would refuse the gift that he would get for me and I said no. He then asked why I would refuse the gift that God wanted to give me. All I could say was oh. Then he began to talk about patience and how he needed some. He proceeded to pray give me patience. I looked at him is that all you are in for now. He could not understand why he was in for it. When we got to this one little road that we had to turn left on, it never had traffic. Well it had traffic that night, and more traffic, Bill is saying hurry up oh God give me a break, were going to be late. Meanwhile I was laughing and laughing. He looked at me and told me it wasn't funny, but I reminded him it was his request not mine. When we made it to the Christian retreat we were a bit late, but the concert was worth every second we were there and the long drive down to the retreat. As Revelation was singing all at once I had some weird words come to my mind. I thought what is that? I didn't say anything I just stood there, they came again and this time I couldn't keep my mouth shut and they popped out. I guess I got this silly grin on my face because Bill looked at me and grinned and said you got it didn't you? I could only grin and nod, I was afraid to try and talk for fear those weird words would pop out of me. I had told the Lord on the drive, if this is of Him and he wanted me to have it okay.

The name of the church was The Church at Tarpon Springs. Richard Brown was a pastor, he had been a Baptist minister until they gave him the left foot of fellowship. And he found this old church in Tarpon Springs and started a church of his own. I loved that little church and the people. The guitar player was named Dennis, he definitely was different from anybody else. He had a monkey which one day was running over all the house roofs in Tarpon Springs. They finally caught the little stinker, and Dennis took him home.

Before I was coming home to Indianapolis one time a group of the people were praying with me that Steve and I could get back together. They told me that if we prayed and believed God would answer that prayer. They forgot to tell me that when you are dealing with another person's will it's a whole different ballgame. That person may not want to do what you're praying for. As much as that hurt me when Steve refused to come south with me, I was devastated I was so sure that prayer would be answer. To this day it has not been answered no matter how much I wanted it know matter how much I asked for it. If another person isn't willing to yield to the wooing of the Holy Spirit, just pray for them, ask God to move in their lives even if you are not a part of it. For me I cried all the way from Indianapolis through Kentucky, Tennessee, and into Georgia because Steve didn't want to come back with me. I have wanted to tell him so often how very, very sorry I am, and that he was a good husband and that it was my fault. Pure and simple. But all I can do is ask the Father to minister to him to save his soul and bless him.

# Chapter 13

$\mathcal{I}$ met a girl from Minnesota. She was asking me to write to this gentleman she knew back in Minneapolis. I refused to do it because I felt that wasn't right for me to write him first. I would see her off and on and always she said the same thing. So I finally told her that he does not know me from Adam and it's not right that I write to him women just don't do that. But she assured me it was okay. I finally relented after much persuasion and wrote to Jeff. I was surprised that I received a letter back so quickly, it was May 5, 1976. I opened the letter and as I read it, something inside me began to open like a rose. As I read the letter I felt such an excitement, I thought now this is really strange what is going on here. I knew he was a Christian and I knew he was going to this ministry where my friend went. I think the girl's name is Patty, but not sure as it's been so many years. Jeff and I were writing to each other in fact we used to laugh and says same or another mailman because it seemed like we kept getting new mailman down in Florida. He started calling me Princess Jane and so I called him Prince Jeff. He decided that he was going to come down to Florida and be with me and I told him I hated cold weather so he moved down in July 1976. I suggested we go down to Bill's Seafood I believe is the name of the restaurant. And we ordered Greek salad and some shrimp. He started talking about us getting married between his bites of Greek bread, and the salad. Finally I at looked him and I said I want to marry you. With crumbs and his mustache from the bread, he asked me to marry. It was not the most romantic way to ask a girl to marry you, I thought it was kind of sweet. We didn't have a ring so he gave me a hot jalapeno stem and that was my ring. I thought he looked handsome with his crummy mustache.

One of the ladies from the Church at Tarpon Springs, had an extra room which she gladly rented out to Jeff. We set our wedding date for September 1, 1976. We were planning an outdoor wedding in the back yard of the home I was renting. Two little girls down the street fell in love with Jeff. He seemed to have a way with kids they all just loved him. So I asked them to be junior bridesmaids I made bridesmaid's dresses as well as my own. My friend Cathy and her husband Bill stood up with Jeff and I has witnesses. The day dawned bright and sunny, but the closer came the time for the wedding, darkening clouds seem to be around us. We pray and we had sunshine, the dark clouds never came any closer and we really had the wedding: complete, even taking Jeff's parents to Pappas restaurant there in Tarpon Springs. My friend Carl sang for the wedding. All in all it was a wonderful day. After we were done eating, Jeff and I headed for Bradenton and Christian retreat. I kept losing Jeff, I would find him he would be feeding the squirrels and the ducks. They also had a beautiful parrot I fell in love with. So when I found Jeff feeding the ducks and the squirrels, I would go talk to the bird. They call me Dr. Doolittle because I'm always talking to the animals. It can be quite interesting talking to animals and to be surprised what they say back to you. After the honeymoon and Christian retreat, we returned back home to Holiday. One thing about Holiday they have an abundance of parakeets, the first time I saw one I thought someone's pet got away but it was nothing to look up at the wires and see it full of parakeets just chattering away. It was really neat to see that and I really do miss them.

Within six weeks there was a drastic change in Jeff, I was wondering what in the world have I had gotten myself into again. This sweet gentle man that I had married was suddenly having angry spells. I went to pastor Richard and talked to him. He asked me one time if I was that hard to live with, I told him I didn't think so. He then said he wanted to talk to Jeff. After he'd talk to Jeff he came back and told me that it was not me that there was a problem with Jeff. Jeff went to the doctor because he was having headaches often on and the doctor sent him to Meese hospital to be checked out. He was working at Innes Brook is a groundskeeper. They took x-rays and certain spot around the brain stem and cerebellum. They told us he had MS. But he didn't really have any symptoms of MS. So Jeff went back to work. One of the girls from church was going back to Indiana and Jeff felt I needed to go home and see the family. So I did and while I was up here I was at Mark and Phyllis's home. I went out to see the dogs in the backyard I had known I believe Randy was the name of the dog, since he was a puppy. So I was talking to him when the next thing I knew his paw was tearing up my eyebrow and my cheek. The next thing I knew he grabbed my right arm. The words relax, move with him, came to me so I did it. Phyllis was standing up by the house holding a 2 x 4. But she was concerned that he might turn on her also. Suddenly Randy let go of my arm, I immediately start heading toward Phyllis as fast as I could but not too fast so as to upset Randy more. I looked at my arm there was a good-sized –gash, and it was bleeding pretty good. Phyllis got me out of the yard, into the house, leaving a trail of blood everywhere I went she grabbed a towel and wrapped it around my arm, and said that we were going to the hospital. We went to Community Hospital and they fixed me up quite nicely. I decided to call down to Florida and tell Jeff that if he got hospital bill to just ignore it that Mark's homeowner insurance was covering everything. But I could not get an answer to my phone calls. I tried later that night, then the next day, then tried the day following. I could not understand why I could not reach Jeff at the house, so I called Pastor Steve the associate pastor. He said Jeff was in the VA hospital in St. Pete. He got ready to go to work, got in the car and started to go down the street. Problem was he lost his vision, it came back enough that he could find his way back to the house which wasn't too hard. The landlord had painted the house a bic banana color if any of you remember the bic banana pens. They were very yellow just like the house but the lasting where I live I would tell them you know that big house yellow color with the blood red trim. Everybody in Tarpon Springs knew that house. My friend Carl was renting the upstairs when he came downstairs Jeff told him he had a problem. He and I had never thought of the VA but Carl and Dennis did as they were servicemen too. So they took Jeff down to the St. Pete VA for evaluation. When I got there I was a mess I had a bandage over my eye a bandage over my cheek, and one on my arm. I walked in and was amazed when Jeff was not surprised to see how battered I was. He's always took everything that way just took it. Just stayed there another week and then they transferred him to the Tampa VA where they used a special dye that they were able to find tumor in his brain.

This occurred in the summer of 77. When Renée had died I told the Lord I never wanted to go through something like that again. The interesting thing was I knew this was a death sentence for Jeff. I kept telling him to ask the doctors what the diagnosis was and what they found but for some reason he wouldn't do it. So finally I told him. Because he kept saying that once the doctors knew they would tell him but they didn't. He took it like everything else just looked down and didn't say a word. They started to plan for his surgery. I knew I was supposed to go make arrangements and I couldn't bring myself to do it. The surgery was cancelled and this happened two more times. After the second time, I asked my girlfriend to go with me and I went to the cemetery for that area with no money somehow we talked the guy into giving the plot with no money down. I left there trying to keep my mouth from hanging open in total shock. Then we went to the funeral home and I made arrangements for his funeral and also made arrangements for mine thinking I was going to be in Florida the rest of my life. After I did that the surgery went through. The doctor came out he was the top neurosurgeon in the United States and I was so blessed to have him be Jeff's doctor. He came to me after surgery and told me they could not get all of the tumor that it was on the brain stem and cerebellum.

They started Jeff on radiation treatments, when he would go down to have his treatment, there were some tiles missing in the ceiling, he told me he would see Jesus sitting up in the ceiling watching him. I thought that was so neat. I had someone tell me that I resented the fact that Jeff was going to die. I said yes I do, why shouldn't I? I marry this wonderful man we have six weeks of beautiful togetherness then he suddenly becomes someone I don't know. I didn't think he would hit me. But the abuse that I experienced was very real to me as to the possibility that it could happen. One day I was pounding stakes into the ground for some tomato plants that I was planting, when all of a sudden he began to yell at me, I knew what was coming next, and I couldn't take another beating. I was in a flashback and did not even realize what I was doing, but I was raising the hammer and would've smacked in the temple, but an angel was there and before it was too late grabbed my arm and stopped me! I was sick when I realized what was happening, I told Jeff to go in the house. He still ranting and raving so I said it again a bit louder. I don't recall how many times I said it, but he finally stopped screaming and carrying on and went into the house. I was raising rabbits at the time I had under the carport and any time I got stressed out I would go and see my rabbits. They were able to calm me down. I went into the house found Jeff and apologized. I don't know how many times the Lord carried me through those days.

In December Jeff wanted to be baptized, we went to a friend's house from the church. They had a pool and Jeff wanted to be baptized in the pool, even though it was colder than Billy Ned and the pool was not heated. I was concerned about him catching cold or something but he didn't. I was going to college and also working for the Suncoast News as a photographer and short news items, as well as trying to take care Jeff. The 19th I believe it was, the Cancer Society had given us Christmas presents, as I had no money to work with. They brought in a hospital bed and set up gaining what assistance they could to help. After the bed was set up Jeff got in it. He would never get out of it. It was a Sunday and I went in to check on him and he kept sitting up and told me oh honey I feel so funny. He kept saying this over and over and over.

Finally in the afternoon he was suffering so bad that I told him just to let go and go to Jesus. He told me that he was ready to go anytime. I put a call into his brother in California and told them if he wanted to see Jeff he needed to get on a plane now. He told me to keep him alive till he got there. I was dumbfounded as the brother is a veterinarian. Well he didn't make it Jeff had already passed when he finally got here. People were not coming to see Jeff and I when he was able to talk and enjoy people. When word got out that Jeff was in a coma the people came out of the woodwork. I kept thinking where were you when he was able to talk to you, when I could've used a break. One brother started rebuking the spirit of death and another brother got caught up in it I couldn't take it. I went to the kitchen and the Lord told me he was taking Jeff. I told the Lord okay just don't leave me, and He didn't. Jeff died on Monday morning 22nd of January. When I knew Jeff was gone, I put on his favorite song Rise Again, by Dallas Holm. I went to the funeral home and even though I had made prearranged plans they went through everything all over again. I thought in taking care of everything there is nothing else to do so I went along with the program and found out that I did not need the cemetery plots that I got because the National Cemetery in Pensacola was able to take Jeff and it would be much cheaper so that's what I did I shifted off to the National Cemetery. As soon as I could I got all hospital stuff out of the house and on the front porch for pickup. I didn't stay at the Big Banana very long as every time I walked to the living room I could hear him breathing. So I decided to leave the house. I was having trouble with my car. It turned out to be the alternator so Carl was changing it and I told him when René died I found if I could find something funny in this whole mess I could make it. But I was hard pressed to find something in it this time. All of a sudden it struck me, Jeff is in heaven walking on streets of gold didn't have a care in the world about a silly car that didn't work and I was so tickled I started laughing. Then Carl and I started talking about the difference between death and divorce and I told him that they are pretty much the same. The only real difference is you know where one is every night. It was hard getting back to the norm, but I knew I had to.

Before Jeff died I made him promise that he would be at my graduation from St. Pete Junior College. As the program began the director of music stood up and made an announcement that there was a special song they wanted to play for the graduates. I like to fall out of my chair when they start playing when the Saints Go Marching In. I knew Jeff was there, that was his song. My friends that went with me for graduation all looked at each other when they heard that song start, and said Jeff is here. That really made my day. I decided to go to the University of South Florida where I got my degree majoring in criminal justice. I thought about going into psychology till I saw a girl who had white mouse in her hand and I asked her about it. She said that the mouse was her maze mouse. I decided I wasn't into psychology.

I had become interested in prison ministry through a couple that attended the church. The man had been imprisoned, and once he got out he started a prison ministry. I got interested in the pan pal ministry to inmates. This was 1978. In 1981 Christian said I needed covering so he suggested that I get my ministerial credentials from Gospel Crusade out of Bradenton. So I was ordained. Over the years I have written to hundreds of prisoners. Most were respectful, but a handful were not and they were cut from the list of people I was writing to. I am still to this day writing prisoners only have one at this point in time. You will understand later why I am only having one person. They would write back and tell me how blessed they were, and I would just think Mercy I know who is getting blessed here it's worth it but there were times I really had to lean on the Lord.

I would go on to graduate from the University of South Florida in 1980. I had done a year of volunteer in probation so

I decided I needed to go to prison to do my internship because I needed to know what these people went through etc. When I graduated I wanted to be a parole and probation officer but there was a hiring freeze on those who had been interned in parole and probation. I was offered a 3030 on the perimeter of the prison. I said no I don't see myself to 3030. So I got a position working as a nurse at Polk Correctional.

# Chapter 15

$\mathcal{I}$ lived in Lakeland and drove over to Polk City to work at Polk Correctional. They housed approximately 1200 men. I worked in the ER triage, emergencies, work camp on occasion, ran the gurney down to the cell house as needed. We had clinics and I helped the doctors. Sometimes I worked in the infirmary. But one day Joe our charge nurse approached me about a new position. I would take off the orders, schedule outside appointments, coordinating security, write out different passes, and as needed schedule labs to be drawn. I enjoyed this position very much I was essentially my own boss and I love paper shuffling. One day Joe came to me and told me that he didn't think I knew how important my position was. I never thought about it, and I told him so, to which he told me I was the hub of the whole medical department, that if I didn't do my job everything would fall apart. Well I became very concerned for my license because of the way the medical department was being run. My favorite left, and the gentleman who took over all he had to do was float around the compound looking good and have his vehicle washed. I wish I had stayed because what I had was an excellent job, this was one of the times when I made a dumb decision.

Even though I had access to see the different crimes that had been committed by different men, if at all possible I did not look, because if I saw a sexual predator I found it very difficult to treat him. We had two inmate orderlies that worked in medical they always escorted us if we had to make a run out on the compound. One in particular that I remember just frosted my gizzard. We got a phone call that somebody in G dorm was having chest pain. They had stayed in just a sweep where they went out and they picked up a whole bunch of people that they decided should be a parole. Most of these men had jobs and they were doing good at their jobs. Most of them are not allowed to go into medication so we weren't sure what they wrote because I couldn't remember the names which caused us great problems **as well as the inmates. I called my two orderlies, they grabbed the gurney so I could open the doors and we rushed out. That's a long way on the compound once and over: for some reason the officers would open the gate that was closer to every-thing coming back but not going down so we had to take the long way to G dorm. We got down there huffing and puffing and the officer came out and informed us that he's not having chest pain after all. Okay what does he want. The officer laughed and said he wants a jockstrap. I looked at him and I said he wants a what? The officer repeated himself I looked at the two inmates with me and shook my head. So we took the way back walking slower this time, got back and one of the doctors asked me where is the inmate? So I told him that he wanted jockstrap he sort of half chuckled, and half snorted as he told me that I have anything to put in a jockstrap. I was so disgusted and out of breath.**

**We had an inmate who loved to go to the doctor. He would do anything to get sent out to the doctors and the hospital. There was nothing wrong with him he was very healthy young man but he wanted attention. He would come in almost every week complaining of something and we could find nothing, so they kept sending him hoping somebody would find something, they never did. Our pharmacist was a long tall black man, the inmates came to the pharmacy to pick up their medications so he had little wind and could see out as he came into medical department and classification. This one day the inmate**

came in and proceeded to fall down the minute he got inside the door. Reggie saw him do it, he shot out of the pharmacy door, snatched the inmate up by giving him a weggie, held him up high enough that he was walking on his toes. All the while Reggie was reading the riot act about all of his faking. He was brought into triage and we had to check him out. Well he was complaining so much that they put him in the infirmary. I was working the infirmary that day and one of the inmates came out of the infirmary and told me that this other inmate was laying on the floor. I asked the inmates that was reporting this to me, how long he had been laying there, because I had been busy up front knowing everything was okay back there. His reply was about an hour. So I told him well when he realizes nobody's coming to fuss over him it will end. Right on cue he gets up over the bathroom door, sees me, grabs his chest and staggers over to his bed and crashes. I could not contain myself I wished I could have had it on film he put all of the drama possible into this act. And I lost it and so did the other inmates in the infirmary. I just looked at him and told him that he was okay and went into the office to do my

One of my jobs was to pass meds in the confinement area which is a small area compared <u>to the cell</u> houses that had two rows of cells the full-length of the room, and then had an office for the officers. You never knew what you were going to see or hear as you walked down the range. One day my officer and I were making the rounds and I heard the shower running so I knew someone was taking a shower. Now the showers are open so that if anything's going on the officer can see it and stop it at that. Confinement is more of a dark hole and you really can't see anything at the shower area. Someone was coming down the range and all of a sudden started calling to me. I'd been nursing long enough that I wasn't the scared kid anymore, so I did the only thing I knew would work. As he was trying to get my attention I looked straight ahead and

**walked quickly, my officer right behind me. Notice the difference from Marion County Gen. where I had no officer with me.**

There was one guy that was doing time and he conned the doctors to give him a walker because he couldn't walk very well without it. But you let every chicken in the cafeteria that day, he would pick up his walker and almost run down the sidewalk. I told the Docs that he did not need that if he's running down the sidewalk carrying his walker. They just waved me off they didn't want to deal with his mouth.

I had come back to Indiana thinking I would stay and I applied for work at what I thought was the new Indiana Reformatory, but it ended up being the old reformatory with the high walls all around it. The guard towers on top of the wall has circular stairs that went out into the tower. If an officer became ill and needed to be brought down it was very difficult to bring him down due to the stairs. One officer decided he wanted to take his chair out and sit on the wall. Only problem was he just fell off the wall. It was a blessing that he wasn't hurt, but every inmate in there just at the sight of this officer on the ground. No one could figure out how he managed to fall, he was not hurt which was a blessing but it definitely offered entertainment for a while.

When you went into confinement was it a totally different ballgame then I had ever experienced. We had to wear, or rather put on motorcycle helmets with shields to go down the ranges of confinement. Sunday I was delivering meds by two officers started on the range. I was sandwiched between the two officers for protection. I did not have my shields down and it was a big mistake that day because this one inmate decided he was going to nail a nurse. He tried to tell me later that he thought it was the other nurse not me. She evidently had done something to really make him angry because he threw what we assume was a combination of urine and bowl cleaner in my face he also got the officer who was behind me and he only had one eye that he could see out of. I backed up trying to get out of the line of fire, and stepped on the poor officer who was behind me. We also turned around and headed back out of the range at that point in time my uniform was soaked, and I needed a change of clothes. But I stopped at the sink long enough to try and rinse my eyes out so they could try to get back to the medical department. They found a red jump-suit and gave that to me and I changed into that and the officers that were with me asked if I wanted to go back and finish I said you bet. I was not about to show any fear or anything else so I finished my rounds looking like a Santa Claus in my bright red jumpsuit. After the meds were done I went to the emergency room and they gave me drops for my eyes after they washed them out. The officer that got gunned down as we call it didn't go to the ER and he was having some problems with his eye. They moved the inmate to the other side of the confinement and back where he couldn't have access to nurses. He kept insisting over and over the down there on the ranges that he didn't mean to get me that he thought I was someone else.

Some people would ask me aren't you afraid to work in the prison. No I wasn't afraid I was just very aware because I knew who it was I was dealing with in there, but also I knew that they respected me and knew I was the real deal. I wasn't going to run games which is very, very important. I never did get to be a parole and probation officer. I tried to get a classification that they can see beyond my nursing license even though I have a degree in criminal justice.

# Chapter 16

$\mathcal{I}$ was living in Indianapolis and I got a call from my friend Ginny. She told me of this new Minister had just come over here from South Africa with his three children and his wife. They only had $300 when they landed, and to me that was using some giant faith. She told me that he was having meetings at Carpenters Home church, and that the evening meetings were filling up the church. Now this church could hold 2000 just on the ground floor not counting the balcony. I asked what his name was and she told me it was Rodney Howard Browne. She said that he was also on the 700 club, so I decided to try and get the 700 club on my TV. It came in so snowy that I really couldn't see much, but I could hear what Rodney was talking about. I was so impressed when I heard him speak that I decided I had to get back to Florida as quickly as possible. So I got myself up and my kitty cats, as I am a kitty person. I was living in an apartment, so I just packed everything up and away we went. The kiddies did very well on their trip next to Florida again. I got down there and got settled. My cousins help me unload and I let the kiddies out of their carrying cases so they could check out the new place. I put in an application to return to Polk Correctional, and it worked out. I was like a sponge at those meetings when I could get there to hear Rodney speak. One night as we were singing and worshiping God we heard the angels sing. It was awesome, I had never heard such beautiful music before. I was so glad they got it on videotape, as I have listened to that tape quite frequently. I went to as many meetings as I possibly could and I could feel myself growing spiritually. When Rodney decided to start a church, I was one of the charter members that was with him at that time. We were meeting at the University of South Florida's Sun Dome. We met in a room called The Coral. I thought it was quite fitting for the church to be in the corral. The mascot or whatever you call it was a Brahma bull. I would drive over from Lakeland to Tampa to go to church. I loved going to church, I couldn't wait for the next meeting. Sometimes we would just praise the Lord for an hour. When Rodney started to speak you forgot the time, it didn't matter what time it was. He just was so anointed that he didn't want to stop. I had never been in a service like that and I was so hungry. (Rodney now can be found on the net. If you are interested to check him out, I don't think you'll be disappointed.) The church, The River at Tampa Bay, is a thriving church and they are reaching many people.

I saw in the paper that they wanted hospice nurses. I had always went to work in hospice. When Jeff was so ill and dying, hospice was in its infancy. Life Path hospice had their main office in Tampa, and they were opening a new office. They were starting up a continuous care unit where we would go out to the patient's home in order to process last five days of life. We were there to relieve the family so that they could get some rest because we knew what they were going to be suffering and dealing with in a matter of days. I enjoyed that work very much. I also worked weekends, where I would go out on visits, and encourage the patient and family. Also if anyone called in for a problem the RN generally sent me out. I would triage the patient and report back to the RN what I found. Generally, I was able to take care of the problem myself, but on occasion the RN would have to make a visit.

I had some interesting experiences. I went to this one home it was a lady who was ill, and her significant other was trying to take care of her. The lady was listed as an dagnostic. Her significant other stated that she was an atheist. We were not supposed to speak to the patient regarding salvation, so

I would just lay my hands on her pray, "Lord, while she has the time, reveal yourself her and give her one more chance". Then I begin to praise him for her salvation. Through that shift she kept putting her upper right-hand in front of her face and pulling up her right leg as if to shield herself from something. She was very, very agitated on that shift, even though I was medicating her on schedule. The death-rattle was very prominent. I shifted her left. The next day, when I returned, I thought to myself that she looked different. Was just my imagination? She wasn't as restless as she had been the day before. The death-rattle had increased even though we had medicated her and she was getting it. Her daughter came in from California. As the daughter and the woman's significant other were at her bedside, the daughter all the sudden exclaimed that she looked so peaceful. I looked again and I inside I was screaming and crying yes! He is faithful and I expect to see her again one day. What a privilege to stand in the gap for soul.

Another case was a 96-year-old woman. She had known the Lord all of her life. It was such a joy to hear and see from her daughter what a blessing she had been all of her life. As we went through the deathwatch, the family shared stories; some were funny and we would all laugh. The family would speak, and also sing to her. As the evening wore on, the daughter prettied audibly said that the Lord would take her home and not let her suffer anymore. Instantly the respirations changed, and we all saw it would not be long. In one hour or two, I listened for her heartbeat. When I heard none, we acknowledged that she was gone. They began to praise the Lord. You could feel the Lord's presence. About halfway through the night the daughter complained of a severe headache and being very tired, she asked that we pray for her. Her granddaughter and I prayed for her. What a privilege to share in a saint's home going. All the family had time to tell her goodbye, including her seven great-grandchildren, who were there that evening.

The next case I realized well into the shift was a gospel singer. He sang and was friends with the top gospel singers,

JD Sumner, the Gaithers, and Elvis. He had his own quartet, and he played the piano like a dream. It was like what was said of Jesus, "can anything good come out of Nazareth". Only this was Mulberry! He wrote music for different groups, but from what the caregiver told me, he could be as cantankerous as an old mule. Yet this proved to be a most awesome experience. Up to this point I had great difficulty dealing with the dead body. When I was nine years old, my stepfather's father died. When we went to the house to see him, my little brother, Moe, raised the casket and touched the body. It didn't bother him a bit that he was cold and stiff. But I did not want to touch him, but I was forced to and I was not prepared for the cold and stiffness of the skin. It really devastated me. Now the rest of the story. I knew we were close to the end of the deathwatch. Chaplin Michael Caine came to visit. As he shared, all once I was so aware of an angel standing off to my right. He was so real I felt I could reach out and touch him. Though I could not physically do that, I knew he was almost to the ceiling in height. I looked his way and smiled. The Chaplin began to sing and the gentleman, Jim, became very restless. Michael stopped singing. We all Joined hands with Chaplin Michael, the caregiver and myself, and prayed over Him. The presence of the Lord was strong. Later that evening, I went into the room. I was on one side of the bed, and the caregiver was on the other. I was aware of an angel at the head of the bed. I looked up and pointed to him where he was. The nodded; she knew what I was talking about. Jim went home peacefully that night. And I had lost my fear of a dead body! Praise the Lord.

This next case was the hardest I think of all my cases. I got the nickname the death Angel, because they would assign a patient to me and before I could leave the office, or get in my truck and start going, they would pass/die, and I would get a call, "don't go, they just passed away". It was rather disconcerting I know; yet very interesting at the same time. There was a young mother with a rare form of cancer which progressed quickly. Silently, she had been dealing with her own death and had not prepared the 10-year-old daughter for her death. I arrived at the end of the deathwatch. Death was imminent and the family came in to tell her they loved her and they would all help with the raising of her daughter. Her husband shared what a wonderful wife and mom she had been, and how she had been so faithful to the Lord. I saw her Bible lying there. I asked her husband if he felt she would enjoy hearing the word. He said yes, so I went to the Bible and read in the Psalms for about an hour. That seemed to relax her. Then when her daughter came in, she was obviously shocked to see me there. I told her that if she wanted to talk and kiss her mom and spend some time with her, please feel free. She went upstairs for a while and then her husband came back down and stayed at the bedside. She finally passed on to heaven, the daughter was in shock. She could hardly cry. Her daddy took her by the hand and led her outside where others took turns holding and comforting her. It was a joy to see the support of that precious extended family altogether for that time. It's important that all children be prepared.

There are many other stories that I can share with you, but I think you get the picture of how work was. We tried to keep the patient comfortable, and support the family so that they could have as much precious time with their loved one as possible. Most families were a joy to be with and I enjoyed my time with them. But just like any place one works, there are also stinkers in mix. There are times when you're having to deal with someone who does not want the person that is ill and dying to be properly medicated. They keep bugging the patient so that they can't have the peace and quiet to go on their journey. I've seen some patients stimulated to the point that they had to go through it all over again because one person would not let them rest quietly, but kept bugging them to the end until they were out of the journey mode. Then, it takes twice as long to make the journey. But you have to take the good with the bad and just pray for them.

# Chapter 17

In 2004 I decided that I needed to move back to Indiana. My aunt Anna Mae had moved in with her children so there was no one in the family left real close. So I packed up Mr. Sunshine, Shadow, and the Queen. I rented a U-Haul and packed it up with the help of my realtor. He sold my beautiful home for a good price, in just a few days of putting on the market; one that I had built there in Lakeland, Florida. I moved up to up to Griffin, Georgia. I thought I had a job there but it didn't work out. I applied at the prison, but they took so long that I was out of money. So, the only thing I could do was to see if the family could help me out so that we might get back home. I put my stuff in storage but some things in my pickup, and of course the babies. We started the long trip, Shadow started yowling all the way through Atlantic traffic until she finally got quiet; it's hard to concentrate in all that traffic. We stopped overnight, and finished our trip the next day getting into Ft. Wayne. I stayed with Lisa until a little house came open and I moved in. I really liked that little house, that was just perfect for me the babies. They used to sit on the little table in front of the window in the kitchen, and on top of to the microwave by the window and they would watch Bailey the neighbor's dog if he was out or the squirrels and birds. For work, I went out to different doctor's offices and made sure that everything was there that should be in the patient's chart: be it for pediatrics or for Medicaid. Since I could not get full-time work, I decided to move up to the Goshen- Elkhart area, where I applied to the

JJC for employment. Madison Center, a mental health center, had taken over all of the Juvenile Justice Centers. The children were sentenced there by the court, where they had 18 months to complete the course. They were trained on how to find a job, how to fill out an application, how to run an apartment, and how to manage your bills, etc. Occasionally we would have one run: they would manage to sneak out past everyone and run away. Generally they were found quickly; sometimes it took a month or two to find them but they usually ended up back in the Juvenile Detention Center.

I was working the evening shift and finding it more difficult to walk. I had no clue what was going on. I just knew I was having difficulty walking. My feet were just hurting so bad that sometimes I just wanted to park someplace. The girl who worked opposite me said she thought I probably had rheumatoid arthritis. I thought she was goofy, so I kept working and suffering until one day I couldn't go anymore; this was 2007. I had gone to my doctor and they had given me different tests. He thought it might be mono, or he thought it was something else. Every time, the tests would come back negative. And I kept on just taking ibuprofen for the pain. I was practically eating it, which is not wise to do as it wreaks havoc with kidneys. I got to the point that I called my cousin and I asked her to come and get me please and take me to the ER. There was no way I could drive there: I had been in bed trying to recoup and I couldn't. I just I didn't know what was wrong. That morning, when I got up, I didn't care: I had to see the doctor. She took me over to the ER, where they took me into triage then the nurse took me back to the ER. I remember sitting in the chair, I remember her starting to push me, because I **was not** awake. The next thing I knew I was on the floor and they were wanting me to stand up. I couldn't; they had to help me stand to get my weight. By the time they got me back to the room where I was to stay, I couldn't get out of the chair as my legs would not hold me. I was in the hospital for several days and I had no idea what was going on. I was dumbfounded when my night nurse came in and asked me if I knew that I was in atrial fibrillation when I came in. I didn't know that, nor could I understand why no one had told me. A doctor came in and was looking at my crazy legs and feet. He drained some fluid off my one knee and told me he'd be back to see me later. Little did I realize that it was going to be a long relationship with Dr. Lockowitz. I really liked him. He diagnosed me with rheumatoid arthritis, degenerative disc, and osteoarthritis of the spine. Several years later, in 2012, I was diagnosed with fibromyalgia. In the same year I was diagnosed with congestive heart failure. It is no fun trying to keep the fluid off of you, as it's a constant battle to keep water down. If too much water it goes into your lungs, that is where congestive heart failure comes in. I have a wonderful cardiologist, Dr. Gonzales, who, as far as I'm concerned, is the best in the area. Dr. Gonzales and Dr. Lockowitz are so great and I appreciate them so much. Well in 2009 I decided to retire. I was so glad to be out of nursing. It took me 47 years to get out of nursing. And I don't miss it a bit. It took Dr. Lockowitz and me five years to figure out what works on my condition. The sad thing is that you try so many different things and they don't work. Then when you see something you think might work, the insurance company doesn't want to pay for it. And they want you to try this and this and this so we played their game. House in such an insurance companies they will not pay for the medication that I have been on for several years. So I have to go off the medication that was working and go to what they want me to try. Neither Dr. nor I have been happy campers.

For a long time I would tell people not to turn 65, for when you do you fall apart! I moved into a residential apartment building for seniors and I really enjoyed it. But I wanted to come to the facility that my two aunts live in. I was finally able to do that last year 2013. My Queenie just really loved it here. I got everything I need; my family takes me to the store to go buy supplies. One really doesn't know how long one can keep that up. My Queenie kept me laughing, as a lot of times she got in this mode of I'm going to pull this rug, and she would. I had a kitty door in the door of my last house leading to the front porch. Queenie would pull the rug through the door. I'm not talking about a small rug. I don't know how she did it without pulling her teeth out at times. One of her favorite toys was the milk bottle rings that you break when you open the jug. She put her paw on the ring and it would stand up. Then she took it and flipped it in the air. Sometimes she would attack it and do a somersault in the process of her attack. That was quite something to see. Queenie escorted me to the bathroom, or anywhere I would go. One day she saw Mr. Sun standing on his hind legs and doing a kangaroo walk across the hall into the bedroom, now Sun was a long lean kitty machine. When Queenie tried this trick her little short legs just didn't work and she fell over so she did not try it again. Though she was quite good at trying to imitate Mr. Sun with a lot of things. Once, Queenie was chasing a mouse. They were in the dining room when I happened on to see Queenie looking down at the mouse. The mouse was also sitting on his hind legs with his little front paws up as if was praying she will leave him alone. I eventually caught the mouse in a wastebasket put it outside so it survived because of Queenie. You ought to try and catch a mouse with a wastebasket sometime; it's really quite exciting. One time Mr. Sun got scared and didn't complete backflip, somehow it startled and scared him. It was too funny to watch. Sunshine every day was watching the birds from the window. He would sit there and be still as he could be. Then when it finally got to him, yak, yak at them. Sometimes Mr. Sun would tear around the house like he was in the 500 race. It was too funny to watch them go. I so enjoyed my kitties over the years; they were like my children.

# Chapter 18

As I dealt with the reality of what I was facing, Rheumatoid Arthritis is a crippling disease, and I'd only seen one case my nursing career and it was horrible. She was almost in a fetal position, legs drawn up and her hands or fingers were so crippled she couldn't even hold a glass of water. They had gone in and done surgery and had pins stuck in her fingers like safety pins on the end, and the baby pins, if you know what I mean. I knew my life would never be the same, and that bothered me. Through the trauma, I prayed and prayed on many occasions, requesting God to take me home to heaven. Then I thought about my precious kittens. I didn't want to part with them, so I decided, cancel that request please. I knew in my heart that God had work for me to do. "Why" was the big question. Had I not suffered enough and lost enough. I lost my daddy at six months old, sexually abused, spousal abuse, was pregnant seven times with only one child living three and half hours, divorced, my beloved husband Jeff dies of cancer after one year and four months of marriage. "Now I have to face this" came to my mind. God's answer was that HE might be glorified. I received the same words when asked about the physical infirmities and pain I was dealing with; okay I do not compute His answer, but I'll give it my best. It was so hard to adjust, that I cried on more than one occasion. Once at a family get-together, I broke down crying "I am too young for this," I was 65 years old. I sent my current prayers and praises to the Lord. Now five years later, I walk with a cane a I give thanks to the Lord. I still feel like Job, who after he had lost everything, the Lord restored it all. And like him I can say "though he slay me, yet will I trust him".

I was feeling very blue one day, and all at once, I looked out the window and this is what I got. I call it God's little blessing, and I want to share it with you. Have you ever just sat and looked out the window, taking in the beauty of God's nature TV? If you do maybe you will notice things you never seen before. I have some physical difficulties because I sit in my recliner inside the window for hours at a time. One day I was amazed as I looked and listened to what I had not noticed previously it was a time when I felt so terrible and I was considering asking God to take me home again. Then I saw my heavenly Father blessing my cat Queenie and I changed my mind. Looking out the window the first thing I saw were the plants, shrubs, and trees that are on the edge of a patio beside my building. The sky was a beautiful blue with not a cloud in sight. The sun was shining brightly. The lilacs were blooming; they looked like in massive limbs hanging down like clusters of grapes. The picture was so sweet and refreshing that I wished they could last all year long.

The Butterflies were visiting the flowers. The Bluebirds, Cardinals, Sparrows, Wrens, Mourning Doves, as well as the old Finches flit here and there, catching both my attention and the Queens... One day much to my surprise a yellow Finch landed on the bottom part of window. The Queen was sitting on the table in front of window. All at once she raised her paw, and the birds flew away. I told her that she couldn't put her paw there as it would scare them.(She has had a Paw problem, as it had gotten her into more trouble such as patting my water glass, and giving me a bath!) The next day it came back, this time the Queen jumped up to the window and off flew the bird. So we had another type of instruction. Again the following day the bird returned and the Queen was the essence of stillness as we watched a little bird fly away on its own. I was in a lot of pain then, as well as having great difficulty in walking. I knew God had sent that little bird; it was special just for me. He returned several days later, and then on the final day return to stay longer on the window, flying away singing as it went. It has not been back since but I will never forget that little wild Canary.

From the apartment I noticed rabbits, black and gray squirrels that would come to visit. They were so cute to watch. One might even see a squirrel chase another. On one occasion when I watched a squirrel chase another, they ran up and down the trees, across the yard to other squirrels, and across the street. I was shocked to see a total of 12 squirrels in a line right behind the first one was that was scampering as fast as she could go. I was so surprised that I yelled out to the first "you go girl", and then they were out of sight. Watching God's nature TV can be very interesting and enjoyable. One never knows what is going to happen in God's nature TV but what I find so special is that He made it for you and me and if you have days like I had, His TV helped me make it through that time. His TV helped me make it through that time, because I know he cares for us all.

I have gotten quite used to my limitations. Some days that I would have a lot of pain, and some days I wouldn't have anything. I was thinking that my medication was working pretty well and it wasn't bad, I just had to adjust to knowing that I can't do things like I used to do. Dr. Lockowitz had been begging me to see a nephrologist for some time. I finally relented and saw Dr. Coursa. When I walked in, she told me she wished I had come sooner. She asked me if I would consider dialysis. I told her absolutely not. That was one reason that I had not gone before, as I did not want to be pushed into dialysis. I had worked dialysis and I'd seen what it does to a person. And I would live my life out to the fullest extent. She then looked at me and said that she had been seen people with my same numbers live six months to a year. I sat there looking at her as she explained that I was only using 9% of my kidneys this point in time. I was able to hold my composure until she left the room and then I began to tear up. I had been in severe kidney failure since 2012, I believe. She did not have any hope of anything but a death sentence. I sat there thinking about what I had just been told. She told me that if I wanted to get hospice involved, it would be okay with her. I decided to wait a little bit see how things would go. I knew which hospice I wanted. As an afterthought, then I needed to go ahead and get everything squared away so that they would be on board and they could pay for some of the medications.

Hospice came in and was asking me about my pain. Now for me to be at eight pain on a scale of 10 is not that bad. I have learned to live with pain about that level, because there's just not anything out there that really helps. So she said it was better talk to the doctor and see what they suggested. I didn't think anything about my sister, who was staying with me. We had gotten the hospital bed in so I could have a bed and my sister could also. I did not realize what was happening but I was slowly being overdosed they told me that I should call my cousins on Grand Island and asked them to come and get my Queenie. She was to go to them when I died. I do not remember making a phone call or anything. Judy was give me the medications as was ordered. Judy is my sister. I remember having all kinds of weird dreams and hallucinations. But as the days went by I was hallucinating more. I was thrashing around in the bed, and I wasn't making sense of the time when others would talk to me. I only know what I was told about what was going on. I have absolutely no memory from the last few days of January to the whole month of February. It was the end of February that they decided to send me to the hospice House and give Judy a break. Once I was in hospice house they pulled back all new medications that I had been taking all long. It took me four days to come out of the drug stupor. I told Judy that she was not taking care of a normal patient; that I was acting like anyone that is been overdosed on drugs. People on drugs are very difficult to deal with, that even in the ER with plenty of people to help, there are times when it's almost more than you can handle because they're so wild and is a strong. I looked up on Friday had been sent there Monday. I saw someone standing beside me and recognized the uniform and knew I was some kind of hospital. I kept asking questions about what happened what was going on. Judy informed me that one time I had gotten up and fallen. That had split my head open in two places, which it took nine Staples close the gash on my head. I don't even remember a thing about it. I was so disappointed when I woke up, and the guy had taken me home. As I was sitting there, I sang a song about I want to go home. I stopped singing and the words to the same melody came to my mind finish the book. I knew I had to finish my book this book.

About every three months the Mast cousins get together for a meal. We just finished eating desert. All at once, Wayne started talking and is looking across the table so I know he's talking. He said" God has something very some special for you to do". I was looking around the table to see who he was talking to, when everyone said he's talking to you Jane. I'm going "o". All the time wondering what in this world I'm supposed to do. So I thought about it and prayed about it. Afterwards, just as I thought about writing about my life, that I've been talking to different people and we talk about things I did in my life and they always say "Jane, you need to write a book". Well I've been trying to write this book for some time but I just couldn't seem to get at it. When I was in so much pain at the beginning part of my diseases, I didn't have the strength to do it. I have found that writing is work. And you can get very, very tired in trying to put your book together, because the person who thinks it might be interesting to read, you want them to read your very best. For all my life I know the Lord has carried me. I could not have made it through all that I have if it hadn't been for him. You may or may not know the Lord. You may be like I was; I knew about Him, but I didn't know him personally. When I came home from hospice house, I found Judy had essentially rearranged everything in my house and some things were not there. Some things were thrown away that I desperately needed and it was so hard to shut my mouth, but I did. I know she meant it to be of help, but it was sort of a shock. But what was the worst was that my Queenie love e I believe it was Jesus and the role of a shepherd ministering to his lamb. He was dressed in a Joseph's coat of many colors. There was a hood on the coat and it was up over his head. He ever so gently put one hand on my shoulder and his arm around me. He didn't say a word, he just ministered to me silently. I could see the concern in wasn't there, and I was devastated. I was in the bathroom and broke down and started sobbing the guttural sobs. All at once I knew somebody was standing at my side His face. I still wanted to get my Queenie back, but she had gotten used to the family and she was adjusting well, and from here to Grand Island was a long trip. So Judy suggested that I tryand find another kitty that needed a home and that's what I've done.

I am at the end of three months, and I can tell changes in my body. I have no idea how long I have, but the Lord promised I couldn't go home till I finish the book. My greatest desire is to leave this earth and go home to be with Jesus. To me when I talk to Jesus and the father God I tell Him like it is. He knows what I'm thinking anyhow, so why not be truthful. I tell them everything, I had to leave Honduras. I had gone down as a medical missionary and I loved it. I loved the people and the land of Honduras. I loved the fact that it was like being back in the 50s. When my funds ran out, and my visa ran out, I had to leave the country. For the visa alone, I had to leave for 24 hours. I was so upset that I couldn't stay. As I was getting on the plane to leave, I was very upset with God. In fact I told him I was not talking for a while because I was so upset. He just waited patiently on me get over my snit I went down with a medical doctor John and his wife Blanca. The flight from Elsalvador to Tuguciagapa was a lesson in faith! It rattled like all of the rivits were about to fl y out of the plane. w this Dr John leaned up and told me we needed to land before dark as there were no runway lights, and there was a 50 ft. drop at the end of the runway! We stayed overnight at beautiful home that wan an embasy at one time. The nest am we left for LaArada, and arrived to a HUGE tranchula!!! Freaky, scary! That was not the only one, I found one behind the barrels we used to get water from the Elsavador border. We did clinicas out in the bush, were we would have people come from miles away. We usually had 1000 + at each clinic. We had to sleep on open porches at times. I loved it! The Lord cares so much about each and every one of us. Just stop and think if you would you be willing to give your son to die on the cross like Jesus did so the world could be saved? I know It couldn't it be too much to ask for me, and I'm sure you feel same. God did give his son to die on that cruel cross because he wanted to be with him forever. All the prophets are saying we are in crunch time. Time is short before the Lord returns and takes those of us who have made Jesus Lord of our life; those who said to Jesus "I surrender to you". If you are not sure about Jesus, asked him to reveal himself to you -and He will. You do not need a fancy prayer or a prayer filled with these thou's etc. There have been times when all I could get out was help Jesus. He heard and He helped.

In the 1960s my mother and I were an automobile accident I ended up in the hospital in traction. Back then if you are in neck traction, your head was at the foot of the bed so they could work that traction better. I was in traction and my neck was spastic and pulling down to one side or the other side. They thought I was thinking so they gave me what they call a placebo injection. I knew almost immediately what they had done and I called him and I told them I need something for pain. As I lay there all of a sudden from the wall that I was facing came this brilliant light, I'm lying there wondering what in God's green earth is going on, so I kept watching. The light got brighter and brighter, suddenly I noticed a figure coming towards me out of the wall. I really thought I was hallucinating. As the figure came out of the wall he had white gown on, he walked into my side and I couldn't take my eyes off of his eyes. His eyes were so full of love and compassion he reached out his hand and took three fingers and lay them on my forehead oh such a tender touch and so cool. I didn't want Him to move His hand. But he did is slowly fading back into the wall and the brilliant light faded also. I began to watch the nurses as they came in to me, they always came from left side, there was no brilliant light involved. When they put their hand on my fore head it was it was with an open palm.

Mom came and I told her the story, she just looked at me and said, "someone is praying for you". And I had to agree with her. After all these years I still remember every bit of that incident, at that time I still didn't know like I do now. It was in the 70s before I found out he really was. So my request of you is check it out, as Jesus wants to make himself real to you. And I want to meet you in heaven one day. I am already praying for the people that read my book. I have no idea how many will split. It is my fervent prayer that you will know who Jesus is like I do. And let him carry you like he has me through all my twists and turns, ups and downs, and doing stupid things. There is one thing about a Christian, a true Christian. We may fall down and land a mud puddle. But Jesus loves us so much he comes to us and picks us up out of the mud and says, "I love you so much: learn from your mistakes, keep short your problem list before you messed up, be quick to forgive yourself and others, and you never can go wrong that way."

## THE END

CPSIA information can be obtained at www.ICGtesting.com
Printed in the USA
LVOW13s0908300714

396608LV00013B/474/P